THE SMART MONEY GUIDE
Unlocking the Secret ESCG™ Code

Janet McGinty & Raymond Aaron

Authorities**Press**

The Smart Money Guide: Unlocking the Secret ESCG™ Code
www.TheSmartMoneyGuide.com
Copyright © 2019 Janet McGinty and Raymond Aaron

ISBN: 978-1-77277-242-5

Publisher
10-10-10 Publishing
Markham, ON
Canada

Printed in Canada and the United States of America

Table of Contents

Acknowledgements

I would like to thank my collaborator, **Raymond Aaron,** for his guidance, insight, and mentorship. Raymond has been instrumental in transforming a good book to a must read.

How did this book come about? I was given the idea to provide a seminar on financial planning, not from the perspective of giving. I gave a great deal of thought as to how giving contributed to wealth. I put some thought into simplifying and giving a framework to help people understand their financial picture. I addressed what I believe are the four fundamental skills of money management. I believe that with clear insight into those skills, you'll have the confusion surrounding your financial picture cleared away. Clarity and awareness will help you move forward with your life design and goals.

I would like to acknowledge my father, **Robert Payne,** for his support. He has set an example for integrity in action and the value of honesty. I would like to thank my late mother, **Shirley Eley,** for helping me develop resourcefulness and resilience. She had a curious mind and was well informed in a time before the internet. I sometimes marvel how she got her information. I would like to thank my father in law, the late **Bernard McGinty,** for the help and support of his family. I would like to thank Kevin for inspiring me to write this book.

I would like to thank my congregation at Eastminister/East End United for providing the inspiration for this book. I looked at finances from a different perspective and developed the ESCG™ to help people clarify their finances.

I would like to thank Mooredale Sailing Club for providing me the opportunity to learn to sail and improve skills, exercise courage and friendship.

I would like to thank my clients that believed in my ideas and abilities. I would like to thank them for providing me the opportunity to learn so many other aspects of business through them.

To my daughters, **Ciara and Brenna,** I would like to thank them for making me the Mother of Miracles. With them, the impossible becomes possible. Every day I am grateful for these two girls. Every day, they motivate me to get up and go. They inspire me to be better and I appreciate their fresh insights and comments. I am so proud of them, and they are the best thing that has happened to me.

Foreword

Have you ever wondered how Benjamin Franklin came to be on the American $100 bill? He's the only non-president featured on American currency. Ben Franklin was born in Boston in 1706 into a family of 17 children. He was not formerly educated by any stretch of the imagination. He educated himself through extensive reading and left home at 17 to go to Philadelphia to go into the printing business. He became a newspaperman, publisher and author. He created numerous inventions: the Franklin stove, bifocals, the catheter and the lightning rod. He's best known for his experiments with electricity. He also researched demographics, meteorology, refrigeration, oceanography and marine travel.

In 1732, Benjamin Franklin wrote, "Poor Richard's Almanac" under the pseudonym, Poor Richard. In its time, the Almanac was enormously successful, selling 10,000 copies. Poor Richard presented himself as a dull, but witty, country character who believed in hard work and simple living. Many of Franklin's most famous quotes are from Poor Richard's, such as "Haste makes waste" and "Early to bed and early to rise, makes a man healthy, wealthy, and wise." The Almanac proved so successful that Franklin continued to write one every year for the next 26 years, selling about 10,000 copies a year.

In 1758, he wrote the essay, "The Way to Wealth," a collection of advice advocating thrift and a strong work ethic. This is considered the first American book on personal finance, and is still considered one of the best and wisest money books ever written. His smart and witty advice advocated hard work, earning and saving money.

Fast forward to the current day. Money and finance continues to confound the average consumer. There are many sources, mixed messages and products. Since the 1700s, the money system has changed, the stock market has changed, and the housing market has changed. The commodities markets have also changed. Technology has changed. It goes without saying that very little resembles the time of Ben Franklin.

We now have fiat currency, Bitcoin, derivatives and credit default swaps. We have investment bankers, quantitative traders, financial engineers and hedge funds. Almost ten years ago, we had a financial crisis that crippled global financial institutions. Deregulation, financial engineering and a disregard for lending due diligence contributed to the crisis. The crisis decimated the finances and savings of many. Have they recovered? Will they recover? What happened to cause the crisis, and can it happen again? What's a bubble? Why do we have them?

Good advice is timeless. The complexity of finance can be undone and the simplicity made readily apparent. Why simplicity? When you can understand and explain something complex in very simple terms, then the transfer of wisdom is possible.

There are many things you can't and won't understand because you just see the end product. You won't see the building blocks of knowledge that built that technology. In finance, you see the end products. You hear the talking heads. You read the news. Everything seems so complicated. It doesn't have to be.

Before going any further, I would like to commend you for choosing this book. It's my belief that you've picked the book because something about it appeals to your situation. While I don't know what that something is, I do know that Janet McGinty can offer you a number of possibilities. She can teach you the ESCG™ Code, which can help you to clarify and understand your financial picture, to make better choices about money and to provide you with some tools to help you get your money working for you instead of you working for money.

Loral Langemeier
The Millionaire Maker

Loral Langemeier is one of today's most visible and innovative money experts. She accelerates the conversation about money, sharing how to not just survive this tough economic climate but how to succeed and thrive.

Introduction

How to read this book? I'm sure you picked up this book with the intent to learn and inform yourself about money. The financial industry has its own language, as do many industries and groups. This serves to let the people in the know exclude the public. It follows that you can give yourself a huge advantage in learning if you read this book with a dictionary on hand, and check words that are unfamiliar to you.

You learn language mainly from context rather than actual definitions. As a result, there are many words that are commonly used but aren't properly understood. Similarly, there are words in the financial industry that are taken as commonly understood, but they aren't accurately understood by the public.

When you pass over words you're unfamiliar with, you may find yourself tired or unable to take in more content. If that happens, back up. Look at the words you paused over. Check the definitions. Even words you think you know the meaning of, check. I've included room at the end of the chapter to write down words to look up.

For words I want to be expressly clear, I've included the definitions. This may seem redundant, but it will help reinforce such words in your mind and help you understand the material better.

This guide addresses the four skills of money management and will provide you with a simple framework through which to view your financial picture. With that framework, you'll be able to clearly identify what you need to focus on.

I believe in your success on your journey of learning and transformation.

Chapter One

Money

"Money is a guarantee that we may have what we want in the future.
Though we need nothing at the moment, it ensures
the possibility of satisfying a new desire when it arises."
– Aristotle

Definition of Money

Noun: money

1) a current medium of exchange in the form of coins and banknotes; coins and banknotes collectively, 2) sums, 3) the assets, property, and resources owned by someone or something; wealth, 4) wealth, riches, fortune, affluence, assets, liquid assets, resources, means, financial gain, 5) payment for work; wages, 6) a wealthy person or group.

Origin Middle English: from Old French *moneie*, from Latin *moneta* (mint, moncy), originally a title of the goddess Juno, in whose temple in Rome money was minted.

The Mystery of Money

It's no secret that many people struggle with managing money. Why is that? Is there some mysterious code or knowledge that some people get and others don't? Why does money management seem so complicated? What's your biggest challenge in managing money? There are answers to these questions.

What is the Origin of Money?

I would like to start with the origin of money. Originally, people bartered or exchanged goods for goods. With this, everything was negotiable. Eventually, to reduce the need to negotiate, a commodity was exchanged, as a measure of value. Salt, tea, tobacco, beef, or grains were trading commodities. The challenge was in the carrying, storage, or perishability of the trading commodity. Metal coins appeared as early as 700 B.C. Countries came to mint currency. Paper money came to replace coins.

Initially, currency minted by countries was representative, meaning the money could be substituted for something. The pound sterling could be exchanged for a pound of silver. Other countries used what was referred to as the gold standard.

Now we're in a system of fiat money, currency declared legal tender by a government. The value of fiat money is based on a combination of supply and demand, interest rates, and perceptions of the government or the national economy. For example, the value of the Canadian dollar is highly correlated to the price of oil.

Money developed primarily to facilitate trade and the exchange of goods and services. Trade evolved from goods for goods, to goods for metal coins, then paper representing metal, to our current conception: goods for notional, or an idea of money—fiat currency—a notion declared legal tender that's backed by a government.

A definition of money is a promise backed by confidence. What does that mean? Money has value because we have confidence that it has value. It's based on mutual acceptance of value. There are several parties: the issuer, the seller of goods, and the buyer holding money. Banks take deposits and issue receipts or statements. Contracts are drafted and negotiated. All parties agree that the currency has value.

Aside from value, money has a future connotation. According to the controversial psychologist, Dr. Jordan Peterson, "Sacrifice is a discovery of the future. You make sacrifices in the present to make the future better." In his analysis, "Money is a promise, which your sacrifice will pay off in the future." You work because you've been promised something of value (money) in exchange for the goods or services you've provided. There's a notion that both parties accept the sacrifice (work), the value of the money, and the stability and permanence of that value in the future.

Along with the creation of money came record keeping, accounting, storage and transport. The banking system as we know it evolved from the Knights Templars system of taking deposits of pilgrims and providing funds at their destination. The Templars provided the first inter branch network.

Morality, Philosophy, or Culture of Money

Your notions of money may have been shaped by religion, philosophy, or culture. All religions recognize wealth and poverty.

Judaism is well known for success in financial affairs. Judaism has strong traditions in education, entrepreneurship, and work ethics. Success in finance is based on responsibility, discipline, and following common sense rules.

In Christianity, there are many well-known phrases: "For the love of money is the root of all evil." "Blessed are the meek, for they shall inherit the earth." "It is easier for a camel to go through the eye of a needle than for a rich man to enter the kingdom of God." Christianity puts a moral spin on wealth and an emphasis on sharing and stewardship.

Islam has *Five Teachings*: Wealth is to be enjoyed but not be a distraction; do not make money doing wrong; Practice charity; God will provide; Giving is the source of prosperity.

Hindus have *Lakshmi*, the Goddess of Money. Two of the four life goals are about wealth: Dharma (duty) encourages Hindus to work hard and earn money to support themselves and their family, and Artha (wealth or property) is about gaining wealth by honest and lawful means.

To quote Buddha, *"Money is like water: try to grab it and it flows away; open your hands and it will move towards you."* Part of religion articulates a view of wealth and conduct in attaining wealth and sharing.

In politics, there's great debate over the distribution of wealth. A great deal of thinking and effort is about the distribution of resources and the role of government ... How to reward entrepreneurship? How to encourage the development of business? How to reward work? How to tax fairly? How to take care of those in need?

Culture also shapes our relationship with and perception of money. Culture dictates values of work, shrewdness, thrift, debt, or generosity. A nationality adjective can bring up an archetype and conception of how someone will behave, react, or negotiate.

Creation of Money

How is currency, money, or cash created? You are likely familiar with the mint or treasury of the government. There's a physical creation of currency authorized by governments. The government issues debt, which is a form of money. Investors, domestic and foreign, buy short- term government debt as an alternative to cash. Banks take in deposits and, then, lend out more than they have deposits. This creates money. If you buy something without cash, the vendor can issue credit. This creates money. A store issues points that you redeem for goods. This creates money. A large public company buys another company using common shares. Shares are a form of exchange. Companies enter into barter exchanges and exchange goods and services. You can write an IOU. You just created money. The money supply is not static, and governments monitor the money supply to expand or contract to ensure the stability of the currency, or to stimulate the economy or to address inflation.

In developed economic systems, most of the money in circulation exists as bank deposits, rather than paper money or coins. Commercial bank lending expands the amount of bank deposits. For example, a bank can take in $1 in deposits and lend out $10. Through this notional creation of money, the banking system expands the money supply beyond the amount created by the central bank. Essentially, there are two types of money in a fractional-reserve banking system: currency issued by the central bank, and the bank deposits in, and loans from, commercial banks.

You might ask, "How can the banks just notionally create money?" The banking system is highly regulated with strict capital requirements. One of the reasons loans are hard to get is that the bank makes money by not losing money. Imagine you're lending money you don't have. If you lose on a few loans, you can still remain solvent. If you lose on many loans, then you are in trouble. That was the crux of the 2009 financial crisis. There were too many bad loans. The financial assumptions for loan losses were wrong. Instead of taking $1 and lending $10, some investment banks lent $30 or more. When those loans went bad, they started selling other liquid assets, which brought almost everything down in value. The financial system needed to be bailed out, and the rules and assumptions were re-evaluated.

Now, before you start to think that the banks are just creating money, remember they are creating loans. Those loans have value. They are a debt to one party but an asset to the bank. Although the fiat system may seem to be creating money, it is still backed by debt assets. That's why it's so important that the integrity of the system—the lender and the borrower—observe their responsibilities.

Hard Currency

Hard currency is currency where there's ready exchange and well-developed trading infrastructure. An example of a hard currency is the US Dollar (USD), or any of the currency trading pairs. A soft currency is where there are limitations on its exchange, or a small market.

Today, we're entering a new paradigm of money. Crypto currency is challenging the notions of money. Authority to create money is no longer the domain of government or banks. Is this a great democratization or a disaster waiting to happen?

Crypto Currency

What is digital or crypto currency? Essentially, these currencies are multi-digit, encrypted tokens that are issued in limited quantity. The use of these currencies is currently limited in use for the exchange of goods and services. Their value seems to be more in the speculation of the future adoption of digital currency as a means of exchange.

What is the difference between hard currency and crypto currency? Hard currency is more like a commodity. For example, if you buy a contract for oil, you don't have an identified barrel of oil, just a quantity of barrels, defined by specifications. You hold a quantity of money in an account, and you do a transaction with a specific amount of money. You don't do a transaction based on the serial numbers on your money. Crypto currency has unique identifiers. Your digital token has a unique identifier, so all transactions are traceable. Money turns over, so you can trace the movement of a token, whereas with conventional money, you can only see the macro data—the GDP (Gross Domestic Product), the flow of money. For a company or person, you can see journal entries, but you don't trace the movement of individual bills.

Crypto currency is issued in limited quantity versus the fiat system, where the supply can expand or contract based on actions of a government or commercial lenders. This is an important distinction for the use of currency, the valuation of it, and the impact on inflation.

The size of the foreign currency market is about $5.3 trillion USD. In investing, cash has been considered the zero risk option. You go to cash when you're uncertain of the value of other investments or you're waiting to make a decision; an investment in cash doesn't make money, but it doesn't lose money.

Now, crypto currency has introduced other options. What is an investment in crypto currency? At this point, it seems to be 100% speculation, rather than a zero risk option. Although the rise in value has been spectacular, it's still small compared to the forex trade of $1.6 to $2 trillion USD in trade per day.

At this time, there are many opinions about the future of crypto currency. *Smart Money* is about being aware, and awareness is achieved by asking questions … What does crypto currency mean for the exchange of goods and services? What does crypto currency mean for the current government-based fiat system, issuing debt and taxation? What does it mean for our banking and lending system? Who will be in charge of the currency? If no one, is this a good thing? Will regulation come into play? Can we trust an entirely computer-based, decentralized system? What are the possible security issues—physical versus digital counterfeiting?

Banking serves to provide protection, as well as storage and transfers. Is protection better or worse through decentralization? Is decentralization safer from hacking than what security banks offer? Will it add to or reduce economic volatility? Will it stimulate economic development or fracture the system further? Will digital currency stimulate the trade of goods and services? Can international trade terms (INCOTERMS) and banking arrangements be replaced with smart contracts? Smart contracts are agreement add-ons that go with a transaction.

The fixed supply of crypto currency is different from the supply of fiat currency. Does a crypto currency of a fixed quantity offer a better solution to the current fiat system, which can be expanded and contracted? If the crypto currency pool is fixed, will it contribute to inflation as the economy grows? Will digital currencies provide price and value stability, or lead to inflation? How does crypto currency affect the value of hard currency?

The validation of transactions is done through mining—a process that uses computers to verify transactions using a complex algorithm. This process takes a great deal of computer processing power and electrical energy to undertake. This would replace the verification process that would be done using people and computers—creating journal entries on bank and company general ledgers. This difference in crypto currencies has important implications. The issues, as I see them, are security (cost effectiveness), transactions (buying and selling of goods and services), transaction processing (mining and reliance on networks and computers), stability of prices (inflation), and the facilitation of business (lending).

What does *Smart Money* think of crypto currency? Institutional investors are divided. Some are calling crypto currency a fundamental change for the future. Some call it a bubble. Some are looking to participate in the upside. Some are looking to profit through a bubble crash through options through a big short.

Description of Money

Why have I taken the time to describe and define money in so many ways? Well, money is so pervasive; you likely don't even stop to think about what it is. And it's many things: a way for you to keep score of your efforts to build a certain lifestyle and net worth; a tally of government debt; and a measure of value for business and trade, just to name a few. At one time, people exchanged food for food and goods for goods. But now there is something esoteric about money. You are led to believe that it's only taught to or understood by members of a special group, or that it's hard to understand.

An important aspect of money is that it's a social construction. It originated to facilitate trade between people. Money involves a collective view of value. Money is founded in trust. Money defines people in status and power.

What is Smart Money?

Smart Money is not money. The term *Smart Money* refers to people who are considered experienced or *in the know*. *Smart Money* refers to the people who might invest in a technology or sector before it becomes main stream. The investment industry may refer to *Smart Money* as investing in certain companies or sectors, as a way of illustrating their hypothesis.

Is there a definable group of people considered *Smart Money*? Yes, and no. Institutional investors, venture capital or hedge fund managers, high net worth people, family wealth offices, public company insiders, or celebrity business people might be considered *Smart Money*. But, no, there's no specific association, group, or fund acting in concert. The investment industry can identify block trades but not specifically *Smart Money* trades. It's just a phrase to make some people seem smarter than others—specifically the people not doing what the Smart Money people are doing.

Smart Money, in my definition for this guide, is for informed and aware people. It doesn't have to be a dollar amount. You don't have to have a certain asset or account size to be informed and aware. I would like to help you identify the skills and components of finance, to give you the knowledge base to be *Smart Money*.

What is the most important thing you learned from this chapter?

Words to look up:

Chapter Two

Money Management

"Wealth is not his that has it, but his that enjoys it."
– Benjamin Franklin

"You must acquire the habits and skills of managing a small amount of money before you can have a large amount. Remember, we are creatures of habit and, therefore, the habit of managing your money is more important than the amount."
– T. Harv Eker

Working for Money versus Money Working for You

I believe that when you're working for money, you're working to pay bills and clear debt. You might not even be doing that. You might just be stalling, paying one bill and leaving the others until you are called about your late payments. You might be making minimum payments and paying a large amount of interest—making the bank happy. You may be spending as a way of making yourself happy in the short term, only to find that your debt problem gets worse. In other words, it's likely that you've lost sight of your financial goals.

What do I mean when I say money working for you? It means you have control of your money, and with control of your money, you're in control of your life; you understand your income and your resources, and you're setting financial goals and taking action to achieve them. This is prosperity.

Money working for you doesn't necessarily mean you're earning more money. There's advice available on making more money through a whole host of means. You could start a small business, get a second job, become a network marketer, or invest in real estate. The list goes on. The challenge with all of the mentioned ways to earn money is that you may have a limited amount of time, and you'll be making more money at the expense of time spent elsewhere. If you have a career or family, for example, you may already be taxed for time. What will be the result of landing a second job or starting a business? When I was presented with a network marketing business to increase my income by $500 or a $1000 per month, it sounded like a good idea, but when I thought about all my time commitments, I decided I could save this amount of money instead, just doing what I was already doing. I wouldn't use up extra time, and I could save $500 to $1000 per month, versus spending an extra 10 hours a week to make $500 or $1000. I have children, and just managing that is hard enough. Money working for you starts with evaluating your current position and evaluating what you need to do. Save money or earn more or simply manage your current money better.

Managing Money Better

You may feel that all your problems will be solved if you just make or have more money. The problem with this kind of thinking is that, often, people who come into money, or make more money, just spend more money and take on more debt. The statistics for lottery winners is that two thirds that win substantial sums will be broke in seven years. Money management is a skill that doesn't necessarily get better with more money. You may just get into more trouble or become broke at a higher level. There are plenty of celebrities and professional athletes who made substantially more than most ever imagine but still ended up in trouble with taxes or bankruptcy. Making more money didn't help them.

Consider this analogy: whether you drive a Lada or a Lamborghini, if you're a bad driver, it doesn't matter what car you drive, you're still a bad driver. You must learn to manage your money wisely. I can help you with that: send me an email at **goals@thesmartmoneyguide.com**.

Intergenerational Wealth

"It's not how much money you make but how much money you keep, how hard it works for you, and how many generations you keep it for."
– Robert Kiyosaki

"Be careful to leave your sons well instructed rather than rich, for the hopes of the instructed are better than the wealth of the ignorant."
– Epictetus

There's a well-known phenomenon of wealth created by one generation is lost or squandered by following generations. Andrew Carnegie coined the expression, *"Shirtsleeves to shirtsleeves"*, meaning where someone starts is where future generations will end up. The Scottish have a saying, *"The father buys, the son builds, the grandchild sells, and his son begs."* It is not uncommon for wealth created by one generation to be almost gone or lost by the third generation. In other words, a fortune made by a grandfather is gone by the time the great grandchildren come into it. I believe people assume their children and grandchildren are learning skills by association. Their family may learn some of the skills but not all the skills that they need to manage wealth (e.g., Earning, Saving, Creating and Giving, or ESCG™). More wealthy families are adopting family wealth offices to ensure that there's some professionalism and structure to preserve their legacy.

What are the Dynamics of Intergenerational Wealth?

The First Generation lives a life of hardship, and is determined to make something better for themselves and their families. They're willing to work hard, make sacrifices, and save diligently to achieve their goals. By their later years, their efforts have paid off: they enjoy a more comfortable lifestyle, with assets to pass on.

Their children, the second generation, grow up witnessing their parent's struggle and understand the importance of hard work. They may live a more comfortable lifestyle, but they still remember a childhood filled with frugality and their parent's long hours working. Because of this awareness, they make sound financial and educational choices that help them build upon the foundation their parents left them. With the advantages given by their parents, the second generation may create even greater wealth.

With the third generation, hardship, sacrifice, or struggle is often not experienced. The third generation may only know a life of leisure and be unaware of the effort that went into providing the lifestyle they enjoy. They may be indulged by parents who want to give them the things they didn't have. They may get the expensive new car instead of an older car when they learn to drive. They may have expensive tastes or hobbies, without a thought as to the amount of income needed to provide those things. This may create an adult dependence on their parents if they don't earn enough to support their lifestyle. Without awareness of the effort and process of earning income and building wealth, it's of little surprise when the third generation squanders what their parents and grandparents worked so hard to build.

Why do I bring up intergenerational wealth? It demonstrates that all money managing skills are important. It also shows that having money doesn't necessarily make you good at managing money. The skills aren't learned by osmosis. Good, old fashioned work, and learning all aspects of money management, is important to build, preserve, and transfer wealth. If there's a family business, work in the business at an appropriate level—learning from the bottom. If that is not possible, it's important for you to have the opportunity to work and learn the value of money.

Financial Management

Where's the best place to learn financial management? Our first example is from our parents and how they managed money. There's a complaint that financial literacy should be taught at school. The tools are already taught: math. Much of financial management is just simple math. It's just the application that's missing.

There are many tools, courses, books, and professional financial planners, all dedicated to financial management. With all the tools available, you still might not manage money well. I think there's a reluctance to start, and that's what I want to address. I want you to learn **four skills of finance: how to earn and live, how to save money, factors in the creation of wealth and the nature of giving. As well I would like you to understand some psychology and how to make better decisions. With these and the code, you will then know how to best make use of your resources to start a financial plan.**

I believe you can achieve a great deal by saving money and managing your financial resources better. I reason that you already have resources or income, you shop and you make choices about financials. You just need to do these things better.

But you might say, "I can't achieve my goals on my income." First of all, have you tried?

Live on what you make or make more. Or, perhaps, you've run into one or more of the common financial management pitfalls. Take credit, for example. Credit is everywhere and should be used carefully. It's far too easy to take out a card and buy something you don't need or can't afford.

Secondly, you have been trained to be a consumer to solve problems. Your first inclination to solve a problem may be to buy something. You are bombarded by commercials designed to sell you things. Yet it pays to stop and really think about your problem. You may already have a solution on hand that doesn't involve new spending.

Thirdly, you may have become a slave to convenience. You may want your problems solved fast: if you're depressed, you want a pill rather than relationships or exercise; if you are not fit, you want a pill rather than diet or exercise; if you want a relationship, you want to have him or her there at the swipe of a phone or a snap of the fingers; if something breaks, it's easier to buy than fix. It's tempting to throw things away rather than wash or recycle. The list goes on. The accumulation of wealth is rarely overnight, but the culmination of activities and discipline over time. Discipline and changing actions become habits. More good habits and less bad habits contribute to success.

The last problem is that you may not know the value of your time. You think that you are saving money doing things yourself when you could leverage the time and talent of other people. That is cleaning your house, doing your taxes, managing your money, while your greatest return on time is doing something else. It may cost more to have financial advisors, but it is worth it.

I'd like to start with your resources and your goals. If your goal is to race cars, you wouldn't want to learn on a $250,000 car. Instead, buy a car you can afford to use to learn racing. If you want to fly, start with lessons rather than buying a plane. I wanted to sail. I started with a membership that provided lessons and access to boats. It was a small action that got me closer to my long-term goal.

Stop dreaming, and start acting on your goals. Act in a way you can afford and manage. Acting towards the goal moves you forward. You're building skills along the way. Since one of my goals is to own a sailboat, I'll need the skills to sail it. I had this vision of sailing, so I took lessons sailing dinghies, which are small craft. On my first go, I reached level one but not level two. I took the lessons again as soon as they came available, which was in May and June. At that time of year, Lake Ontario is cold and very windy. So I learned to sail in completely different conditions, with lower water temperature and higher wind speeds.

When you start sailing dinghies, sailing in high winds is frightening. These boats tip over; in close haul, you hang off the side to keep the boat from going over, holding on to a rope, with your feet under a strap. And, eventually, you do tip over, and the water is cold. Or you fall in the boat, or lose control of the rudder and spin around. I also discovered, under the right conditions, you can sail backwards. When you are learning to sail, mistakes happen.

The people that take sailing lessons early in the year are serious. You have to really want to sail, to learn to sail on Lake Ontario in May. I didn't feel like I was as good as my peers, so I decided to go for race training. I had no expectations or intentions to race. I went for race training, I crewed, and we were winning. I didn't expect to race, but it was fun and a great way to learn the same skills. I met some terrific people. In doing something I didn't expect to do, I had this feeling of success and fun and joy that was so worth it. I know I would have been the last person my instructors would envision racing, yet I put myself in training. If a middle-aged woman can learn to race, anyone can put themselves in the boat. You have to put yourself in the boat, over and over again. You have to tip over. You have to make the mistakes. You have to take it to the limit. That is where success is.

> *"Without continual growth and progress,*
> *such words as improvement, achievement,*
> *and success have no meaning."*
> – Benjamin Franklin

> *"Ever tried. Ever failed. No matter. Try Again.*
> *Fail again. Fail better."*
> – Samuel Beckett

What's your heart's desire? If it's travel, start planning your trip. Set up a jar. If it's real estate, start. Go to seminars. There are many real estate clubs. Is it a marathon? Start running.

I believe that you first need to draw a well-defined financial picture—identifying your resources and setting goals. Start with the basics. Master them, and then move forward from there.

You may feel that finance is a mystery, that there's a magic formula or that financial management is complicated. Not so. There's a whole industry dedicated to this. There are many financial advisors, many products, and many software packages to provide projections that tell you what to do. So, why do so many people not take the first step?

Fear and Your Inner Voice

"Do the one thing you think you cannot do. Fail at it. Try again. Do better the second time. The only people who never tumble are those who never mount the high wire."
– Oprah Winfrey

The answer to the previous question is *fear* …

- Fear that you're doing something wrong and will be judged.
- Fear that you'll have to make lifestyle choices you don't want to make, and that you'll be eating beans or camping under a bridge so you can buy mutual funds.
- Fear that you aren't equipped. For example, you may have a belief that financial planning is something you need to be taught. You were taught the basic tools: math. It's up to you to apply them.
- Fear that you aren't worthy, that finance is just for wealthy people, that you aren't going to achieve your goals, and it's better to not know your financial truth. Ignorance is bliss.

"Fear defeats more people than any other one thing in the world."
– Ralph Waldo Emerson

I could go on and on about fear. But the simple fact is that fear is a feeling, which mastery of a skill can defeat. Remember the first time you got behind the wheel of a car. You may have had a great deal of fear. Now you can drive effortlessly. You had to master your fear, and you did so by mastering the skill.

I'll never forget one of our early sailing lessons, where our young instructor told us on a windy day, "You have a 100% chance of capsizing, but we're going to send you out anyway." Out we went. Some of us capsized and some of us didn't. At the end of the lesson, we weren't afraid of capsizing anymore. We knew what to expect and, more importantly, that we could handle it.

One of the major fears we all have is of criticism. The best quote I've read on criticism is by Theodore Roosevelt, and it's known as *The Man in the Arena,* from the speech, *Citizenship in a Republic,* delivered at the Sorbonne, in Paris, France, on 23 April, 1910 …

"It is not the critic who counts; not the man who points out how the strong man stumbles, or where the doer of deeds could have done them better. The credit belongs to the man who is actually in the arena, whose face is marred by dust and sweat and blood; who strives valiantly; who errs, who comes short again and again, because there is no effort without error and shortcoming; but who does actually strive to do the deeds; who knows great enthusiasms, the great devotions; who spends himself in a worthy cause; who at the best knows in the end the triumph of high achievement, and who at the worst, if he fails, at least fails while daring greatly, so that his place shall never be with those cold and timid souls who neither know victory nor defeat."

When you go to do something, there's always that person who has something negative to say. Sometimes it's someone close to you. When my daughters would come to me and say something like, *"She* called me this," or *"So and so* said that," I would simply reply, "Does that make it true?" They would stop, and whatever sting those words had, they went away.

Here's the worst critic … I suspect there's a voice you have in your head. That voice tends to replay negative things you've already heard. *You can't manage money. You don't understand math. You don't understand investments. People in the investment industry and finance are just smarter and better than you.* And so on.

One of the reasons you may have struggled financially is your inner voice. If you hold on to the negative things this voice is saying, then you're giving yourself permission to fail. When you say, "I'm not good at math," you're just giving up on math. All that it takes to be good at something is time and effort. When you see someone master a skill, like an athlete or a musician, you see the result. They make success look effortless. But the truth is they did that performance with a great deal of effort—practice, coaching, personal sacrifice, and persistence. You don't see that in a three-minute performance or routine. You have to put the effort in to master the skill.

To deal with your inner critic, accept the following: You will make mistakes. A mistake is only a mistake if you don't learn anything from it. Success is often just the culmination of mini-failures. Accept making mistakes, but learn from them.

"Do not fear mistakes. You will know failure. Continue to reach out."
– Benjamin Franklin

"Focusing on learning, as opposed to how others view you, changes your primary concern to one of continuous growth. If you're a true student, you won't consider mistakes as 'failures.'
They're simply learning opportunities."
– Simon Sinek

"It's how you deal with failure that determines how you achieve success."
– David Feherty

Change

"When you're finished changing, you're finished."
– Benjamin Franklin

"The mind is everything. What you think, you become."
– Gautama Buddha

I am sure you've heard the expression, *"people don't change."* It's the worst cliché because it's so untrue. Your whole life is about change, from the person you were, to the person you are, to the person you're going to be. There are endless phrases, products, and technologies about change, so how did this cliché come to be so pervasive? Well, there's safety in the familiar. So you may tend to resist change. You also see and focus on patterns, so a pattern that's obvious is appealing to you. Obvious is what you know, where change is about the unknown, about the not so obvious. If you can accept that there are possibilities and opportunities within the unknown, then change becomes more appealing. It also helps to understand that change is a process, not an event. It is the culmination of many mini-steps.

Mastering Skills

> *"Energy and persistence conquer all things."*
> – Benjamin Franklin

When you're making changes, and you have a positive plan in your mind, some people will still make negative comments. For some reason, there will be that one person who finds fault with everything. I haven't stopped being surprised when this happens, but I don't let it stop me. I like to think of criticism as a catalyst. Sometimes, when someone challenges me, I like to think it makes me stronger, as an element in steel. The difference between iron and stainless steel is the addition of alloys that make the iron stronger. Criticism can motivate. Minimally, you can't let criticism stop you. Be proud of attempting change, because that is more than most will do. Praise yourself if no one else does.

To the point of math, I'm good at math, but that wasn't always the case. My grades in math, in my final year in high school, made me decide to go into the arts rather than the sciences. How I got to be good at math was by working as a waitress in the student pub. I wouldn't write things down, so it forced me to remember orders and do math in my head. It wasn't a degree or course but simply doing math. After that experience, math clicked for me.

I have taught myself other things in math, like investments and real estate financials, and tools in excel. I liked the challenge, but later I enjoyed the windows it opened for me. I would look at the mutual fund and stock market, and it interested me. I did my securities course and eventually started working in the financial services industry.

You learn to read stories with your parents holding you. There are positive associations and memories with reading. Math is just another story. People who understand financials are reading a story about what is going on in a company or a property or the economy. The numbers and ratios fall into place for them. Based on a few simple criteria, they know what is going on. You know it's important, but somehow you struggle with it.

When my daughter Ciara was two, I was reading her a book on counting. I asked her a question, and she looked wide-eyed at me and then she said in a very concerned voice, "Mommy, you have to learn." As if I didn't know how to count. She thought that I was relying on her, a toddler for the answer.

I became good at math by doing addition and subtraction in my head as a waitress. I learned to create short cuts and then more advanced skills just got easier. The math you'll use for finance will have been taught in middle and high school. You have tools. You have a calculator on your smart phone. You have access to the internet. You just have to turn your attention and interest to math. You have the tools; you just have to master the skill.

But … my family thinks … or my followers think … or the social network thinks … or my friends think … Stop right there! The people who know and love you have known you in your original state. Don't let their preconceived ideas stop you. Instead, focus on changing your ideas and skills. People's perceptions of you will eventually change. Besides, if you truly have a desire or passion for something, someone's opinion shouldn't matter.

Another you don't plan financially is lack of clarity. You have many messages bombarding you. There are messages to consume; there is easy access to credit; and there are endless shows and social media outlets depicting how to dress, cook, and decorate. These messages serve to give material expectations and show you how to spend money that might be beyond current means. It's great to aspire. It's also great to enjoy and appreciate what you have.

"It is the eye of other people that ruin us. If I were blind I would want, neither fine clothes, fine houses or fine furniture."
– Benjamin Franklin

Priorities

*"Don't tell me where your priorities are. Show me where you spend
your money and I'll tell you what they are."*
– James W. Frick

*"You must gain control over your money
or the lack of it will forever control you."*
– Dave Ramsey

*"It is our choices that show what we truly are,
far more than our abilities."*
– J. K Rowling

If you're in debt, is paying it off your priority? Are you just making the minimum payments? When shopping, do you set an objective or do you buy stuff you don't need? Do you use credit for your benefit? Or are you paying 20% interest, contributing to the bank's profit? Are you part of the retail numbers stock analysts speak of during the holiday season? Is being in debt a way of life for you?

Being in debt just means you don't get to set your priorities; your lender does. Consider the following story …

There was a young man walking down the street who happened to see an old man sitting on his porch. Next to the old man was his dog, which was whining.
The young man asked the old man, "What's wrong with your dog?"
"He's lying on a nail," said the old man
"Lying on a nail? Well, why doesn't he get up?" exclaimed the young man.
The old man then replied, "It's not hurting bad enough."

Are you carrying debt just because it's not hurting badly enough?

There are many books on finance. It seems to me that you picked up this book with the intent to solve a problem. I think, at some level, there's some dissatisfaction with your life and money; and through this book you hope I can help you with some practical aspects, as well as personal satisfaction. This, in itself, is a step forward. There'll be many more steps forward and many exercises to help you get yourself on track.

Procrastination

> *"Remember, a real decision is measured by*
> *the fact that you've taken new action.*
> *If there's no action, you haven't truly decided."*
> – Tony Robbins

As the last reason for struggling with finances, I will address procrastination. I believe procrastination stems from a feeling that you won't succeed at something. When I find myself procrastinating, I just ask myself this question: "Do you think you will succeed at this?" I usually give myself an honest answer. This helps me decide to move forward and get things done. Or it helps me set things aside or delegate things I don't think I'll do well. Sometimes the best thing is just not to do it and get someone else to do it.

There's a reward in new effort. With any new endeavour, there's learning, there's challenge, there's sacrifice, and there are mistakes. In changing, there's often criticism, both constructive and destructive. In making a decision to change, at least you won't be a cold and timid soul. And at best, there's a whole new world of possibilities. Just keep reading.

> *"Believe you can, and you're halfway there."*
> – Theodore Roosevelt

What is the most important thing you learned from this chapter?

Words to look up:

Chapter Three

Modes of Decision-Making

"Minds are like flowers; they only open when the time is right."
– Stephen Richards

What would you say was your best decision? What would you say is your greatest regret? I thought I would start this chapter with a discussion about decision-making because I believe it's important for you to make yourself aware of how you make decisions. There's a great deal of psychology at play in finance, and I've found that having a simple framework helps me assess where someone is, concerning making their decisions.

The main modes of decision-making I've observed are:

Emotional – the person makes decisions based on emotions, such as fear, greed, trust, or love.
Analytic – the person makes decisions based on research, numbers, or data.
Mindset – the person makes decisions based on a unique personal perspective.

As mentioned, there are several ways people arrive at decisions. And in my experience, while people tend to have one dominant mode, generally, all modes are included. For example, everyone needs to feel trust before they do something. Trust is the pre-eminent emotional component of all interpersonal transactions. And everyone needs to do a modicum of analysis or due diligence. That indicates receptivity and interest. When someone is interested, they will ask questions and explore the proposition. Finally, everyone has a mindset and a framework of experience and ideas that shape parameters of what they understand and are comfortable with. This might include personal values. This might include experiences. When you look at people, if you don't appreciate their different frameworks, you can have a great deal of misunderstanding.

To illustrate what I mean about mindset, if you bring up politics, everyone has an opinion. If you bring up investing, people tend to have ideas about investing. If you do a business presentation, you'll be presenting to people who may have preconceived ideas about your proposition. This is the mindset at work. It may not be the primary way they make decisions, but it's how people tend to approach situations. They come with their experience which affects their mindset.

People exist in windows of what they will and won't do based on their framework of core beliefs. People have ideas about investing, where the price of oil or gold is going, whether there's a real estate bubble or if prices are going to continue going up, and if you can make a fortune in crypto currency or it's a total scam. Without even knowing the facts, in many cases, people have pre-set ideas, and these ideas shape how they view opportunities. And sometimes people express interest in an opportunity but, based on something in their mindset, they can't move forward.

I had one client who expressed interest in a certain type of real estate transaction and, after looking at numerous deals, still couldn't move forward. It wasn't until I spoke with an employee about what things were like in his home country. Then I could appreciate the fact that he didn't have faith in the financing and title process. We take these things for granted, but in his country, these things were full of risk. Part of his mindset was a distrust of banks and title.

If you are selling, when you appeal to that person's dominant mode, you'll be more successful. That being said, I believe most sales appeal to emotion because it is effective with the largest number of people and in getting people to act.

Emotional Mode

When you're in emotional mode, you're making a decision based on fear, greed, trust, excitement, stress, or happiness. Many of our life decisions are based on emotion: falling in love, getting married, having a child, adopting a pet, or buying a home. A great deal of the stock market and other markets have well documented emotional patterns and behaviours. Many investment or business decisions are made based on an emotional pull, a gut feeling, or liking someone. Venture capital can get pulled into a story or invest based on emotion or liking management.

> *"I will tell you the secret to getting rich on Wall Street.*
> *You try to be greedy when others are fearful.*
> *And you try to be fearful when others are greedy."*
> – Warren Buffett

Emotion is a powerful force in the stock market, and the patterns of investor behaviour are well established: it determines market confidence, euphoria, bubbles, and irrational exuberance—and the opposite—lack of market confidence and pessimism. It's worth understanding the impact of emotion on investing. Emotional investing will have you chasing returns or pushing the panic button and selling to alleviate anxiety. The liquidity of the stock market makes it too easy to react to market changes or the news.

Understand this about professional investors. It's not that they lack emotion. They read the same newspapers and hear the same media newscasts as you and I. They're getting their emotional buttons pushed. But they also listen to investment analysts and economic forecasts. Through training and discipline, they've just learned to control their emotions.

Emotion is a powerful force in business as well. Venture and investment capital often values the potential of a project based on the powerful feelings generated by a presentation. Without grabbing an investor's emotional investment, it can be difficult to get a monetary investment. The presentation and value proposition may just come off flat and uninspiring. Passion is a desirable quality in entrepreneurs.

Then you have the media. The media and marketing thrive on emotion, and it's a major reason the patterns of investor behaviour are so established. When times are good, the media can encourage people to excess, and when things go bad, the media can exaggerate the negative.

Emotion is effective with charities and can be a powerful motivator to help. Where a spreadsheet on the number of people affected will be accurate, it won't be effective in soliciting funds. Giving, based on emotion, is very powerful.

Politics is a major arena for the emotional mode. Understanding people, and their hopes and fears and motivations, is often the basis of politics. Politicians have to be very skilled in inspiring and motivating voters.

Emotion is a powerful tool in motivating and getting people to act. If someone is predominately appealing to your emotions in investments, then he or she may not have done enough research, preparation, or due diligence. He or she will tend to overstate return and understate risk. Social entrepreneurship, environmental, and humanitarian causes can have powerful emotional appeals, but they may be used to promote a less than optimal investment. Look past the emotion for merits if you are making an investment.

What's the bottom line? Emotion isn't a bad decision-making mode if you're aware that this is why you're making a decision. What is good about the emotional mode? Emotion has intuition. Intuition is the brain's way of making a decision quickly. It isn't analytic but is surprisingly accurate. Emotional appeals are motivating and often get people to act. An effective leader knows how to motivate people, and that often means appealing to emotions.

What's bad about the emotional mode? If you're being manipulated, this isn't a good thing. When I say manipulated, your emotions are being distorted or exaggerated, or a pitch is told to maximize emotional impact.

Exaggerated returns can appeal to greed, but the result is disappointment when the returns aren't as expected. There can be an appeal to get in before it's too late; or the reverse, you're made to feel more fear than necessary. In sales, fear is the most powerful selling emotion. You can see how this can play out in politics and the media. How many fear messages are you bombarded with? Fear and the breakdown of trust is destructive in many respects. Too much fear and people react and act strongly. Out of fear, they may do things that seem irrational.

Many sales are based on manipulating your emotions, with regret as the outcome. Decisions made on trust can turn toxic if trust is violated. Emotion can get out of hand, and people can find themselves doing things they wouldn't normally do, or that they regret doing.

"Fear, greed, and hope have destroyed more portfolio value than any recession or depression we have ever been through."
– James O'Shaughnessy

Analytic Mode

People operating in this mode of decision make use of analytics like spreadsheets, return on investment, financials, market research, or engineering. Analytics like to do extensive research. If you want to sell to analytic people, then emphasize projections, data, and research. Accountants and engineers tend to be high analytics. Professional investors tend to have been more discerning and have higher due diligence demands.

What is good about the analytic mode? The decisions made tend to be better informed.

What is bad about the analytic mode? There's a propensity for indecision and analysis paralysis. Analytics may just analyze and over analyze, and not do anything. After spending too much time analyzing, they may just get bogged down in details and just not act or come to a decision.

Mindset Mode

"We don't see things as they are; we see them as we are."
– Anais Nin

A person in mindset mode is a world unto himself or herself. You have a set of core beliefs that you come with. These may be coherent and well-founded, or these may be based on situational factors or unique experiences. Essentially, in coming from North America, we have a shared sense of beliefs that you might not be aware of. For example, we may share ideas about rights or a belief in justice, because we've grown up with a fairly well-developed body of law and justice system. In North America, we may take the banking system for granted. People coming from outside of North America may have an entirely different experience with such core institutions. This can make someone's decision-making incomprehensible if their mindset is very different from your understanding. When someone is coming from a mindset decision-making mode, he or she may be very difficult to understand unless you get to the core of their mindset.

As a rule, if I find someone confusing, I make a mental note that there's something in a person's mindset that I don't yet understand. In cases like this, you can only understand by talking through the situation and getting to know that person and their history better.

I have also come across people who have mindsets that hinder their ability to evaluate opportunities and move forward with their goals. I have encountered mindsets that believe the stock market is a glorified casino, that personal development is for fools run by scammers, and that real estate is full of problems with tenants and maintenance. I have encountered mindsets that believe only millionaires can give financial advice, and that financial advisors are just glorified sales people. These kinds of mindsets can absolutely prevent someone from moving forward in any of these areas. To a great degree, these mindsets can be more self-destructive than protective.

Now, a mindset is problematic when someone applies the words, *all* or *always*. There's always the possibility that the mindset is true in some circumstances but not in all. The person is using the mindset to shield themselves from experiencing something bad that likely happened in the past. We've all had something happen that we regret, or that was unfortunate or bad. Some of us will evaluate and move on. Some will create a mindset founded in failure. That's a shame.

What is good about the mindset mode? The mindset of an individual sometimes generates brilliant or disruptive thinking: think Steven Jobs or Elon Musk. An individual can come up with an idea or product that can create important changes. They can be great leaders. Mindsets founded on success and positive thinking can be very effective. Optimistic people are more enterprising and willing to act.

What is bad about the mindset mode? Someone in the mindset mode can ignore very important factors, risks, and realities. Someone may lack some of the skills to execute their grand idea but believe that his idea will carry all the water. Someone may ignore or override good advice that might help his proposition. Someone may have a terrible idea and just run with it. On the *Dragon's Den* or *Shark Tank*, you may have seen the Dragons or Sharks advice an individual to abandon folly. The individual got so caught up in his or her idea that important market feedback was missed.

One example I saw was someone who reinvented cigarette packaging so that smokers would not have to touch the filter with their fingers. I don't think this was top of mind for smokers or cigarette companies as a concern, so where was the market? Who was going to buy this solution? This is an example of an entrepreneurial mindset that perceived a problem and put a great deal of effort into something that was not going anywhere. In his mindset, he perceived a problem that wasn't a problem for enough people to make a market.

> *"When defeat comes, accept it as a signal that your plans are not sound, rebuild those plans, and set sail once more toward your coveted goal."*
> – Napoleon Hill, *Think and Grow Rich*

If you want to change your decision-making, then you might first consider what mode you're making your decisions from. Also, if you understand these modes, when someone's selling you a product or investment, you can see what mode they're appealing to.

Awareness in each of the modes will improve decision-making. Know your reasons. Moving your finance decision-making to tangibles—data, numbers—will help you make informed decisions.

Emotion, analysis, and mindset are all part of a person's decision-making process. All together they make a great team. The important thing is to be aware of your decision-making and process, and make sure it's appropriate for your decision. If you're predominately emotional, do more due diligence. If you're predominately analytic, understand you need to act. If you're coming from mindset, do some research and flesh out your ideas with advisors, or build your team to fill out the skill set.

What was your best decision?

What is your biggest regret?

What is the most important takeaway for you in this chapter?

Words to look up:

Chapter Four

Money Personality

*"Money has never made man happy, nor will it,
there is nothing in its nature to produce happiness.
The more of it one has the more one wants."*
– Benjamin Franklin

*"A wise person should have money in their head
but not in their heart."*
– Jonathan Swift

*"Wealth consists not in having great possessions
but in having few wants."*
– Epictetus

I've found that psychology is a really important component of understanding people in finance and investments. Part of the training I received as an investment advisor was in psychology and personality. I'm a more introverted person, so I tend to listen more and let people talk. People open up and speak with me about personal problems more than they might with other advisors. I've read some books on the topic, but much of what I am going to write about is from personal observation and criteria that I've used to help me assess and help people with their plans. I'm not a psychologist, so I wanted a system to help me assess people. For example, in dealing with clients, it's useful to observe some of the personality characteristics that relate to people's relationship to money and finance. These characteristics do have an impact on your finances. People often ask me about problems they have with their mates. Money and differences in spending and management are a big source of problems in many marriages. As a parent, I've been observing and guiding my children, watching their personalities and skills evolve.

In short, I think it's worthwhile to examine some of the personality characteristics I've been able to identify. I find these characteristics are on a spectrum, and they should be considered as the ends of spectrums. People will not necessarily be at the end of the spectrum. You might want to consider where you are and how they affect your financial decisions and goals ...

- Saver/Spender
- Planner/Spontaneous
- Enterprising/Negative
- Generous/Selfish
- Assertive/Passive
- Conscientious/Feckless

Saver/Spender

Savers are the people who read sales flyers and plan their purchases. They tend to be motivated by sales or value. They are happy saving money and may find spending stressful. They might stock pile at sales or put a great deal of effort into couponing and saving endeavours. Further out on the spectrum, savers can be cheapskates or misers who cause problems in their relationships by being socially inappropriate. At the extreme, they may be hoarders, and that presents a whole other challenge.

Saving money comes easier for savers. They have their challenges. They may buy just to save money—buying quantities they don't need or picking up things because they are cheap. They may like high end or luxury items but will be very conscious of the price.

Spenders pick up what they want and buy it. They don't look at the price. They tend to be more impulsive and may be quick to use credit. They may use shopping to make themselves feel better or as a form of recreation. They may have a closet full of clothes with the tags on. At the extreme, they can spend themselves or their family into financial problems. At the far end of the spectrum are spendthrifts who, left to their own devices, may spend into bankruptcy or burn through their inheritance.

Planner/Spontaneous

Planners like to prepare and plan. Planners like to have itinerary and may put effort into preparations. Part of preparation is often to save money. Discipline and patience are easier for them. Delayed or deferred gratification is the ability to resist the temptation for an immediate reward, and to wait for a later reward. Generally, delayed gratification is associated with resisting a smaller but more immediate reward to receive a larger or more enduring reward later. Delayed gratification is important for many plans and goals.

To achieve most long-term goals, you often need to make sacrifices, putting effort towards something that you might not see realized for years. Some examples are education, sports, your career, and financial goals. Planners may put so much effort into planning, that they delay acting.

Spontaneous people just go with the flow. If they forget something, they buy it. They're more prone to act, which can be beneficial. At the extreme of this spectrum is impulsive, which are people who just act on any impulse they have. Too spontaneous may be simply feckless and, in the extreme, spontaneous impulsive behaviour can be self-destructive or dangerous to others.

Enterprising/Negative

Enterprising people are optimistic. They're curious and interested in opportunities. They see potential. They look at problems with a view of finding a solution.

Negative people can find fault or problems in almost everything. They tend to withdraw from, or avoid opportunity. What they see is aggravation or problems, and they may have a hard time getting past these views. They can have a negative spin on just about anything, even things that many perceive as good. They may complain about everything. Negative people can have a hard time moving forward with their goals because, even though they want something, they get overwhelmed with the problems. Difficulty making a decision that you think they want to make is fairly typical with a negative person.

Generous/Selfish

Generous people like to give, and sometimes their giving is their way of getting love or fulfilment. It sounds well and good, but generous people can get taken advantage of; or, at the extreme, they may become martyrs or hurt themselves by simply giving too much.

Selfish people tend to equate receiving with love. Children, by nature, start out selfish; but with maturity, they should outgrow it. Selfishness in adults is a sign of immaturity. At the extreme, the too-selfish person generally has difficulty with relationships. Being selfish can lead to overspending because the person doesn't have the restraint or maturity to see how acting in self-interest affects others. In the extreme, selfish people may see others making money, or achieving success, as their loss.

Assertive/Passive

Assertiveness is the quality of being self-assured and confident. An assertive person will express his or her position, desires and opinions. An assertive person will initiate and maintain effective relationships, be able to compromise and make decisions.

Aggressive is the bully, the confrontational, the demanding without compromise.

A **passive** person is more driven by approval by others. A passive person may believe in fate or luck or that things are out of his or her hands. A passive person is more hesitant in making or may defer to someone else making decisions.

Passive aggressive is indirect resistance, avoiding confrontation, procrastinating, not making decisions that need to be made or losing important things.

Conscientious/Feckless

This is the responsibility spectrum. A conscientious or responsible person wants to do what's right, especially in work or duties—thorough; attention to detail. **Conscientious** people like to pay bills on time and take responsibility for actions and mistakes. They are time conscious, showing up on time and adhering to deadlines.

Feckless or irresponsible, lacking initiative or strength of character, a feckless person avoids bills and responsibility. He may put forward inadequate effort, give many excuses or have a good enough or terrible attitude. He'll demonstrate poor judgement or engage in risky behaviour. He may blame others or circumstances, rather than take responsibility for actions or mistakes. He may be ineffectual, unable to deal with problems, or create more problems than solve.

I use these characteristics to help me evaluate people, their motivations, and actions. It's hard to get people to plan, so understanding personality can help you motivate or avoid problems. For example, with negative people, if you bring up risk or problems, you are going to just make them withdraw more or shut down. You need to emphasize the positive. With positive people, they're easier to motivate, but you might go over the due diligence section a bit more, just to make sure they are truly onside and won't regret their decision.

There are many theories and tests regarding personality. There are even more personality traits and characteristics, but I've just addressed the ones I feel are important for you to be aware of, so that you understand the effects of personality and decision-making with respect to personal finance.

When hired by banks, I did personality tests and one thing I was told is they could tell that I had moved myself on the introversion/extroversion scale. In university, I made concerted efforts to do things to overcome shyness. It is possible to adapt your behaviour if you know something about yourself. Awareness is the first step in change. If you're a spender, you can become a saver. If you're negative, you can learn to become more enterprising.

Your Money Personality and Your Partner

The differences in managing money, spending, and goals are some of the biggest problems in marriage. How does this happen? From my experience, it is easy to get along with anyone when you have no responsibilities together. But add a mortgage, combine incomes, and have children, then that's when all the personality differences come out. How do you deal with responsibilities and setting goals?

What is the biggest challenge with money between you and your partner?

What is the quality you like the most about your partner?

What does your partner talk to you about the most with respect to money? This probably indicates what is most important to him or her. Does he talk about bills? His priorities might be *conscientiousness and responsibility*. Does she talk about retirement? Her priority might be *security and the future*. Does he talk about what would be fun to do? *Fun.* Does she talk about how she needs more money to buy stuff for the house, the kids, etc.? *Lifestyle.*

What does your partner show you the most? Is it houses? Is it sales or discounts? Is it vacations? Your partner might be showing you what makes him or her happy. People tend to do and show what makes them happy, thinking that it makes you happy too.

How to Deal with Your Partner

> *"They say marriages are made in Heaven.*
> *But so is thunder and lightning."*
> – Clint Eastwood

She might want the tiny jar of French Dijon mustard from the specialty food store and he might want the 3 litre plastic tub of yellow mustard from Costco. This may seem trivial but these are the kind of things that drive couples apart. If you and your partner understand the differences in your thinking and personality, you can establish each other's strengths and support weaknesses. One may be really good at saving money, but this person is also the person who has a hard time letting go of the purse strings and having fun. The spender might have seemed fun when you were single, but with kids, a mortgage, and bills, the spender becomes a liability. You can prepare your case to present to him or her. For example, if your mate is negative, you can emphasize the positive. If your partner is a saver, you can emphasize the savings.

Respecting Differences

Once you understand yourself, then it's easier to see people for what they are. You have to have respect for each other for who you are. For example, once you perceive a fault, this may be all you see in your partner. To combat this, begin to look for and emphasize the opposing trait. For example, if you think your partner is selfish, look for times he or she is generous. Failure to deal with problems between a couple in this way can lead them to manifesting themselves so much that love and respect get replaced with criticism and contempt.

Goals

You need to be able to talk about goals and come to some kind of agreement. It's important that you have goals together and a plan to work towards those goals. You have to be able to cooperate and compromise.

Marriage represents a transition from *me* to *us*. If you can't make that transition, it makes it very difficult for a marriage to survive.

Change

People can change, but it takes effort. Change starts with awareness. What I suggest you do is read further for the ESCG Code™, do your sheets separately, and then come together to compare and discuss. Part of that conversation might be about your differences in approaches.

Rules and Agreements

Often, couples or families think they have mutual understanding, but the divorce statistics suggest that they don't. Rules are very helpful for establishing clear guidelines and principles for conduct. You can establish rules for just about anything. Simple is best. Use something, put it away. If you use it, wash it. Rules help establish habits.

Do you find yourself and your partner having the same argument? After an argument, come to an agreement and write it down. It doesn't have to be complicated: establish who does what, how much you can spend without talking to your partner, who shops, how you make investment decisions.

This plan also works with children. Setting guidelines or rules is very helpful in setting expectations. There doesn't have to be consequences. Often, knowing that one has broken the rules or agreement is sufficient to get back into step.

If you would like help here, just contact me for samples, at **goals@thesmartmoneyguide.com.**

Money Personality and Children

With children, their personality is still emerging, and your goal is to help them develop what you believe to be successful personality traits and skills. How you mold developing personality is through teaching skills. One of the first interpersonal skills taught to children is sharing.

Sharing teaches them to trust, how to distribute, a sense of fairness, and how to maintain relationships. Other interpersonal skills include communication, problem solving, negotiation, decision-making, patience, responsibility, conscientiousness, and assertiveness. When you look at all of these skills, parenting seems like a tall order.

As your children develop, you will see personality traits in them. Some children are very much like a parent and others not at all. Their personalities emerge and change; and as parents, we cultivate positive personality traits and skills. Our goal is to help them become successful and productive.

How to deal with children? I've found using positive words can make a difference. Use the word, *contribution*, instead of chores. Stress responsibility. When they ask for something, ask them what they intend to do for it, or suggest something you need done. Saving: cultivate a savings regime. When they get money, ask, "How much do you need to save?" Suggest they equate their savings plan to 10% of their earnings. Then, give them opportunities to earn some money.

Be generous with praise. You are more likely to get what you want from your children if you praise them when they do something you consider to be *right*, or *almost right*. Control criticism. Any parent knows this is easier said than done.

> *"Criticism, like rain, should be gentle enough to*
> *nourish a man's growth without destroying his roots."*
> - Frank A. Clark

I have also observed their negotiation skills. My children know how to talk to me to get what they want. They contrive little business cases. They know to mention that something is on sale. My younger daughter came to me to negotiate a raise in pay on jobs, and came up with a list with prices for jobs. It worked.

To teach kids about spending wisely, I think it is best to let them make some choices, some of which are going to be less than optimal. Sometimes they will learn by making mistakes. For example, I prefer that my children earn and spend their own money. My daughters begged for a toy that after expressing my misgivings, I let them buy, and it turned out not to be the quality or the fun they were expecting. That was a mistake I was willing to let them make to learn value. I will buy what they need, but if they want something above that, it comes from their money.

Learning to earn is a very important lesson for children. Earning fosters appreciation for money. Establish an allowance based on a work schedule, or pay for performance of certain tasks. Establish what you'll pay for and what they pay for themselves.

When you go out, rather than buy them what they ask for, teach them to budget by giving them money you expect to spend, and let them manage it. So, if you go to an amusement park, and you allow them to budget their money, then they can't come back when they have spent it all and ask you for more.

I believe in frank discussions about money. When I'm not comfortable with shopping or the cost of something, I tell them. I tell them what my reasons are. I tell them what I'm focussing on or what obligations I have. As they get older, I have shared what things cost.

At the risk of seeming really old, I will tell you of my early experience. I went to university at the age of 17 and my father just turned over the money that had been saved for me and told me that he expected me to manage and budget. So I did. There were no threats or a lecture. He simply set expectations. I got part time jobs and was self-sufficient from my first year. The goal should be to make your children responsible and self-sufficient. He set the expectation and that was enough for me.

"Educate your children to self-control, to the habit of holding passion and prejudice and evil tendencies subject to an upright and reasoning will, and you have done much to abolish misery from their future, and crimes from society."
– Benjamin Franklin

"Tell me and I forget. Teach me and I remember. Involve me and I learn."
– Benjamin Franklin

Money Personality and Your Parents

In many cases, your parents shaped your views of money. If not your parents, then there may be circumstances in your early development or childhood that affected your view of money. Just reflect on their personality and habits, and how it may have affected you and may continue to affect you. Reflect on your earliest encounters with managing money. Sometimes you will see a similar pattern. Sometimes you will see a pattern reacting to your parent's habits.

Now that I have addressed decision-making and personality, I will move on to the Code. The Code is intended to lay out the components of personal finance so that you can set goals and work with your financial resources effectively.

What could the Code possibly be? Some secret formula? Read on.

What is the most important thing you learned from this chapter?

Words to look up:

Chapter Five

The ESCG™ Code

*"Annual income twenty pounds, annual expenditure nineteen six,
result happiness. Annual income twenty pounds, annual expenditure
twenty pound ought and six, result misery."*
– Charles Dickens

The ESCG™ Code

What I've developed is a code that outlines the skills and areas
needed for managing money. This will give you a framework you can
use to understand your financial picture. It's meant to help you clarify
your goals in each of the areas, and help you focus on the ones you most
need to address. The four points of the code allow you to establish your
framework and goals to develop a financial plan.

"Wealth is the ability to fully experience life."
– Henry David Thoreau

Earning

Earn: verb

Earning: a gerund (a form that is derived from a verb but that
functions as a noun), in English ending in -ing, or present participle.
1) (of a person) obtain (money) in return for labor or services. 2) (of

an activity or action) cause (someone) to obtain (money). 3) (of capital invested) gain (money) as interest or profit. 4) gain or incur deservedly in return for one's behavior or achievements.

Origin Old English *earnian*, from a base shared by Old English *esne* 'laborer.'

The first of the four points in the ESCG™ Code is earnings. Notice, I didn't call this section *budgeting*. In business, the stock market focuses on earnings, which is essentially the revenue of the business less the expenses. Stock price is often based on what is called an earnings multiple. Essentially, the bottom line of business is earnings: how much profit you have left over after all of your activities.

You will do the same. Your focus is to be on earnings. This is not your salary. Salary is your sales revenue. Earnings are what you have left after living expenses.

The goal of life is not to just to survive, but that is exactly what a great deal of the population is doing. Many people aren't even surviving but are just going further and further into consumer debt. Poverty is *not covering survival or living costs*. Extreme poverty is *starving or working to death.*

Under the earning section of the code, I look to business. Business leaders set goals. Accounting sets budgets. I want to approach your life with leadership and goals. Once the goals are established, then setting the plan and aligning the resources is much clearer. Set the goals, and then adjust the accounting.

Saving

Noun: saving; plural noun: savings; plural noun: one's savings, adjective: saving

1) an economy of or reduction in money, time, or another resource. 2) the money one has put aside, especially through a bank or official scheme. 3) preventing waste of a particular resource.

Origin Middle English: from Old French *sauver*, from late Latin *salvare*, from Latin *salvus* 'safe.' The noun dates from the late 19th century.

With credit, the discipline of saving has gone by the wayside. As a financial planner, I wanted every cent I had invested. I didn't see the value of savings. I didn't think it applied to me because I was a professional. But the truth is that saving is an important skill and a solid component of your finances and assets.

You might say credit gives you the same result as saving. It doesn't. Credit is a liability. Money in the bank, however, is an asset.

Creating

cre·ate: verb, gerund or present participle: creating
bring (something) into existence.
cause (something) to happen as a result of one's actions.

Origin Late Middle English (in the sense 'form out of nothing,' used of a divine or supernatural being): from Latin *creat-* 'produced,' from the verb *creare*.

The reason I call this section, *creating*, is that, through investments, you're creating wealth. Your money is working for you. You may have a job and a salary, but by investing, you're leveraging your abilities and your time. Your money is working for you with investments.

I put investments after savings for a good reason. You need to go through the process of saving and not jump ahead. Savings in investments is important. For example, in real estate, you can improve the value of your property dramatically by just reducing your costs.

Giving

Give: verb, gerund or present participle: giving

1) freely transfer the possession of (something) to (someone); hand over to.
2) bestow (love, affection, or other emotional support).
3) hand over (an amount) in exchange or payment; pay.

4) used hyperbolically to express how greatly one wants to have or do something.
5) communicate or impart (a message) to (someone).
6) commit, consign, or entrust.
7) freely devote, set aside, or sacrifice for a purpose.
8) cause or allow (someone or something) to have (something, especially something abstract); provide or supply with.
9) concede or yield (something) as valid or deserved in respect of (someone).
10) allow (someone) to have (a specified amount of time) for an activity or undertaking.
11) predict that (an activity, undertaking, or relationship) will last no longer than (a specified time).
12) carry out or perform (a specified action).
13) state or put forward (information or argument).
14) pledge or assign as a guarantee.
15) present (an appearance or impression).
16) yield or give way to pressure.

Origin Old English *giefan, gefan*, of Germanic origin; related to Dutch *geven* and German *geben.*

Notice there are many different meanings to the word, *giving*. Giving is such an integral part of our life, psyche, and well-being that it warrants examining. You can't breathe without giving carbon dioxide in exchange for oxygen.

You may say, "*I want to build wealth, not give wealth.*" But it's very important that you understand the nature of giving. There is more to creating wealth. Giving looks at how and why you are creating wealth. Life is more than surviving. Your foundation for building wealth is based a great deal on what was in place and given. You also build wealth for yourself and to transfer to your family. You participate in a community and through our taxes and charitable donations; we shape the community we live in. If you have children, you give a great deal of time and money to raising young people.

Much of what you achieve is through *negotiation* or discussion aimed at reaching an agreement. In negotiation, you give or offer something of value to receive something of value. The job applicant gives an account of why he is the best candidate. The employee gives effort and time for wages. The business person offers a value proposition to customers or potential investors. Building a company or team entails giving financial incentives and acknowledgement to talent. Life is full of many small negotiations of value and giving, whether you recognize them or not.

If not negotiating, you give effort or time to pursue goals that you don't realize for a long time. Often, you see the results of success but not what that person did or gave (or gave up) to receive those results. Giving has the most different definitions and is integral to wealth, but in ways that are not obvious. It is an important skill.

Much of the world is in poverty. It is shocking that so much of the world is in extreme poverty and, at the same time, there are such extreme pockets of wealth. Money doesn't solve problems. People solve problems, sometimes with money. Many problems aren't being solved, even though a great deal of money is put towards them. With giving, you can be more effective and contribute more with measurable results.

The Four Quadrants

To work with the ESCG™ Code, take a piece of paper and fold it into four quadrants and write the words: **Earning, Saving, Creating, and Giving.** Under each heading, write down your related goals (without numbers—just words in each section). Then, read on for more details …

"Financial peace isn't the acquisition of stuff. It's learning to live on less than you make, so you can give money back and have money to invest. You can't win until you do this."
– Dave Ramsey

"The greatest gift of all time is that you can make creation infectious because people spend less time being negative... If you log all the time with negativity in the while world, I wonder how much better the world would be if people sat down and did something positive. It spirals."
– Skrillex

Of the 4 parts of the Code, which do you think will be the easiest for you?

Which do you think will be the most challenging for you?

EARNING   **SAVING**

CREATING   **GIVING**

Words to look up:

Chapter Six

Earning

"Your greatest asset is your earning ability.
Your greatest resource is your time."
– Brian Tracy

"Earning is a product of learning.
You're only one letter away from earning more."
– Richie Norton

Goals versus Budget

In business, the focus of a company is on the bottom line—earnings. How much is left from revenue after expenses? The value of the business as a stock price is based on a multiple of the earnings. This is the way I would like you to think.

You may have a salary. That's your earning power. Your salary might be $50,000 or $150,000. It would seem that the person with the salary of $150,000 earns more, but that might not be the case when you look at what is left over after expenses.

A company is asked by investors about *burn rate*. The burn rate is how much money the company is spending each month. I would like you to think that way. What is your burn rate? By adjusting your burn rate, you can have higher earnings at $50,000 than someone who earns $150,000. The trick is to keep your expenses in check. At the end of the month, if you have money left over, you've earned money. Most people focus on their income or their salary, and not what the results are. If you were in business, the main focus would be on the bottom line—earnings—which are the net result of sales revenue less expenses.

In business, to improve the bottom line, you can increase revenue or you can reduce expenses and become more efficient. In this respect, if you do need to adjust your living, you can increase your income or cut your costs. By setting your goals, this will help you align the choices you make with your resources.

One of the aspects of financial planning that is always brought up is the notion of budgets. I have found that a word can make all the difference in a person's receptivity. That's the reason I won't use the word, *budget*, or tell you to set one at this point. I think that is one of the reasons people don't set budgets. It defines their life. Goals open up possibilities. Use a positive word, and it makes a great deal of difference.

What I'm suggesting is that instead of setting a budget, set your goals and what you want to do. You have a certain amount of income and resources, and it is only sensible that you live within your means.

Before you can begin to manage your money, you need to clarify what's important to you. Write down what's important to you, and use your list to help you decide goals for your money. I don't believe your goals or life have to be determined by numbers. We are continually presented with numbers, like a salary. That number defines you. On a $50,000 salary, you can only do certain things.

The secret to building wealth is very simple: live below your means. Focus on after expense earning. That's it. The bigger the difference between what you earn and what you spend, the sooner you'll find yourself with enough money to do what you want with your life.

"I look at my annual budgets for everything and anything, and I look to see where I can save the most money on those items. Saving 30% to 50% buying in bulk—replenishable items from toothpaste to soup, or whatever I use a lot of—is the best guaranteed return on investment you can get anywhere."
– Mark Cuban

Now, I realize that "live below your means" may sound trite. That doesn't make it easy. When you look around and see what other people have and do, it may seem hard. Realize this. Many of the people you think are wealthy, with big houses and luxury cars, are in debt and just covering payments. There's an illusion of wealth that can easily disappear with a job loss or interest rate change.

For you to build real wealth, you have to set your own goals. If you want to keep up with such people, you can only fall into the same trap. Real wealth comes from spending less than you earn, again and again, month after month, year after year. It's a slow and steady process. It isn't particularly exciting, but it is the surest way to reach your biggest financial goals.

Companies always have limited resources. There will always be more projects, opportunities or capital expenditures vying for the company's money. A company may have multiple opportunities, but everything in some way contributes to the main objective—earning.

Regardless of your financial circumstances, you will have the same experience – more possibilities or opportunities than money. Once you reach a new plateau, you get used to it and then start envisioning new possibilities.

Fixed versus Variable Expenses

It's a good idea for you to understand some accounting principles when it comes to finance. Fixed expenses are those that you have to pay—essentially to live. These expenses are your rent or mortgage, utilities, debt and insurance. These expenses are generally set and not very negotiable. Variable expenses are those that you can affect. They may be essential to living, like food, but you can have some impact on your food costs. Transportation, cell phone plans etc. Discretionary funds are what is left over for savings or investing.

There are two numbers that you should calculate. One is your basic fixed expenses per month. The other is your variable expenses. Together, these form an estimate of your monthly expenses. You should review all of your expenses, but the variable expenses are easier to change. There are guidelines as to what is suitable for your income for housing. Start with your current financial situation. Find out where you are and then you can set your discretionary targets and figure out what you need to do for earnings and savings.

Wants versus Needs

I believe this is another concept that just sets people up for failure. If you're in survival mode, you absolutely need to separate wants and needs. Survival mode is just meeting costs of living. And it's very likely that you aren't even meeting the bare standard of living.

If you aren't buying the staples of life, you're buying what you *want*. So, in that respect, almost everything is a want. So, by categorizing wants as acceptable, you give yourself permission to indulge your wants.

What you do need to do is establish reasonable expectations and priorities for your situation as it is now. What characteristics are most important to you? What choices can you afford?

Now, you may think, "I've set my goals," and now you are limiting with, "What can I afford?" I didn't say this was a book on magic. My father-in-law had an expression: "Champagne tastes on a beer budget." Everyone has limits. Even the wealthy are careful in how they spend. A luxury car can range between $75,000 and $250,000 or more. Wealthy people will establish what they want and what they are willing to spend. When they go to a dealer to buy a car, they don't say, "I would like to pay more for this car; how much over the list price are you willing to take?" Everyone haggles. Wealthy people are careful how they spend their money. They like bargains and discounts too.

I like nice things. You like nice things. There are simple ways of making compromises to get what you want at lower prices. I will say that you'll need to apply a little bit of effort. Sometimes it is just as simple as doing an online search to compare prices or check for sales.

There's another expression. "Fake it 'til you make it." This is often used by people to justify overspending. Take the first two words, *"fake it."* What if a pilot said, "I'm going to fake it?" Or a surgeon said, "I'm going to fake it." For who is it alright to be fake? Even the word reeks of deceit, and I think you get the point. Relationships matter. Instead of faking it, set expectations, and then meet or exceed.

I was in a business networking group, and a participant approached me for business financial planning. He presented like the perfect prospect. He needed a business loan and a group benefit plan. It turned out that he was too perfect and, I came to conclude he was a faker. The problem was, it wasn't just me. Several people presented me with a scenario where they met this fabulous prospect and how things were going well and then it just stopped. They were confused and at a loss. He did this enough times to enough people that he developed the opposite reputation. I am not sure what his goal was, but I think he was living the *fake it fantasies* at the expense of many good people, creating confusion and wasting time. Lying diminished his credibility and reputation. Acting out fake it fantasies will just make you a better actor.

Now imagining and visualizing are effective tools to motivate and help you attain your goals. Imagine honourably. Rent a luxury car for a day. Go to the car show. Drive through neighbourhoods or go to open houses. If you want to visit France and can't afford it, go to a French restaurant. Have dinner on a boat cruise. Follow the stock market. What you can do is enlist a realtor to source properties and you can engage an investment advisor to come up with a pre authorized purchase plan and share your goals. Write them down. Now you have allies interested in seeing you achieve your goals and helping you chart a productive path.

If you are actively working on goals, you can write down goals as if they have been achieved. This can be a helpful neurological practice. It helps your mind think you have done something. It can reinforce your confidence to tell yourself that you have done something that you really want to do.

Confidence is important. Creating a good impression is important. Do you really think you're going to get a client or a job because of the car you drive or the suit you wear? Most of these decisions are based on confidence in your skills and the relationship you cultivate. Your attire and car will just confirm what someone thought, not change their mind.

I am not saying that creating a good impression isn't important. There are ways of getting nice clothes or a luxury car at a lower cost. No one asks to see the receipt or bill of sale, so you're the only person who needs to know what you paid for something. Successful people aren't turning their cars over every six months. A lease is 3 to 5 years, so you don't need a new car, just a nice car. You can shop online for clothes or through discount retailers to achieve the results you want.

A big determinant in getting clients is by building trust. I believe there's a simple formula to getting people to trust you. It's to be trustworthy. That means being authentic. Build your confidence in your skills. Skills don't get coffee spilled on them or dinged in the parking lot.

Increasing Your Income

You may have made a career choice that means you're on salary. You may feel, based on your goals or personal situation that you need to increase your money coming in. So, what you might consider are ways of bringing in more money. There are a variety of ways you can do this and several considerations here.

Time, Skill, and Resources

Time: if you're working or have a family, how much time can you dedicate?

Skill: often, sales opportunities are presented, and selling takes skill. Network marketing is very popular. Sales take time, and there are calls to be made to get the leads to get the sales. A popular business is selling online, which takes some time, money, marketing, and computer skills. Investing is a skill. You might be able to bring in extra money with your job skills: writing articles; doing taxes; or doing renovations, if you're handy.

Resources: if you have a home, you might rent out a room or basement apartment. If you're staying at home with your children, you might mind other children. There are part time jobs online that require skills that you have. With a little creativity, there are many opportunities.

Saving Money to Improve Earnings

Rather than making more money, you can also consider saving money. When a company is mature or large, or not able to grow its business or sales, it typically looks to become more efficient, or looks for cost savings in operations. Saving money means reviewing your expenses as to where you can make reductions. It also means that you are more diligent in your variable expenses—reducing your food or clothes costs.

Reduce Your Expenses

I've come to realize that this is a skill that's not well taught. My mother was extremely frugal, and it used to drive me crazy. In her childhood, times were tough. She was raised on a farm, and her family, like many, had a lot of children. The war and the depression affected their generation in their thinking about money. It created a generation of very practical and thrifty people. When things got tough for me, I really appreciated that I had her sensibilities for saving money.

One of the first things you can do when it comes to saving money is to reduce waste. Our culture is very wasteful. Being careful about waste is the first step in being mindful about expenses. You can then get into being careful with shopping and expenditures.

There was a time when I had extremely limited resources, and two children. I had to be very careful with my money, and I was very diligent about what I did. I sometimes look back and wonder how I did it. I made it work. Kids were fed, clothed, and entertained on very limited means.

They would ask for things, and I would just set that as a goal and think of a way to make it happen. One summer, my daughter asked to go camping. As a single mother, I thought about how I do this. The next week at church, they announced a camping trip. So, I thought, I can get some equipment, and if I need help, there will be people. So we went camping. I got the basic equipment, but I didn't have a stove; so, we just ate foods that came chilled in the cooler for a weekend.

Then she asked to go to overnight camp. I looked into it, and *for-profit* camp was expensive. I found there were *not for profit* camps at less than half the price. These camps had what I was looking for: bunks, outdoor activities, etc. She went and enjoyed it.

My daughter asked for an expensive brand of track pants. I went to the store, but they were $80. I told her that I could not afford them from the store. Later, we found them at a thrift store. Was she happy? Yes. Did anyone ask to see the store receipt? No.

Now if I set a budget and had a budget mindset, I wouldn't do certain things. Whatever goal or thing I wanted, I focussed on making it happen in a way I could afford. I looked at it as a challenge, and there was always a way to achieve it. I set the goal, and then the finances to fit the goal. It can be done.

"Too many people spend money they earned to buy things they don't want, to impress people that, they don't like."
– Will Rogers

"The happiest people don't have the best of everything; they just make the best of everything."
– Unknown

Set Your Goals and Priorities

You have the power to choose what's important to you—positive cash flow at the end of the month, or debt. If you lack focus on your financial goals, it's very easy to give into whims, advertising messages, or reality show standards, and overspend. Goals are your targets, just like in business, and they'll help you align your resources and build your plan.

To summarize, in business and your life, there are basically two things you can do. You can increase revenue, or you can reduce costs. To meet your goals and finances, what do you need to do? Do you need to make more money or save more money? It's that simple.

If the goal is to increase your income, how much do you need to increase it by? What can you do? Rent out a room, drive for Uber, or rent out your car, get a part time job, do network marketing, work in online sales, or invest in real estate. By setting up a small business, you may have additional tax savings and deductions. The income generated in a corporation may be lower than the income generated by your salary. If your goal is to save money, what amount do you want to put away? From there, I can suggest strategies. For example, what is the best scenario for you to improve your earnings? Calculate fixed and variable expenses. Calculate your monthly income. What are your monthly earnings (income minus expenses)? You may contact me for ideas on saving money or making money, at **goals@thesmartmoneyguide.com**.

What is the most important thing you learned from this chapter?

Words to look up:

Chapter Seven

Saving

"If you would be wealthy, think of saving as well as getting."
– Benjamin Franklin

"The habit of saving is itself an education; it fosters every virtue, teaches self-denial, cultivates the sense of order, trains to forethought, and so broadens the mind."
– T.T. Munger

Why Savings Are Important

With the rise of the credit card culture and low interest rates savings, the discipline and skill of savings has gone by the wayside. As of 2017, the average Canadian has about $22,000 in credit card debt. That amount of consumer debt is just crazy. If just minimum payments are made, this means about $4,000 in interest a year. This is the nail that should hurt if you are in this situation.

Savings are important, for example, so that you have money for emergencies. Other reasons for saving are peace of mind and putting you in control of your finances. Then there's discipline. The discipline of saving will set the stage for other areas in your life. When you are disciplined in one area, it follows suit that you are disciplined in other areas.

Saving is not a get-rich-quick scheme. Patience is important to get you through the slog and routine of most endeavours. When you save money, it helps you be more discerning in your financial choices and purchases. You will be careful because saving money is hard.

Attraction of Money

There's an expression, *"money magnet."* You may have heard of the book, *The Secret,* and *the Law of Attraction.* Well, in my experience, nothing's more attracting of money than money. There are idioms ... *Money in the bank ... Cash buyer.* Why are these so powerful? It means you have resources to act. And money attracts money. People bring opportunities to people they think have money, not to people who have credit, or who are broke or in debt. More opportunities will give you more chances to create wealth.

Law of Accumulation

From *The Secret,* many people are familiar with the Law of Attraction. *The Law of Accumulation* was proposed by Brian Tracy. *"Every great financial achievement is an accumulation of hundreds of small efforts and sacrifices that no one ever sees or appreciates. The achievement of financial independence will require a tremendous number of small efforts on your part."* Essentially, wealth is the result of many small actions rather than one big act. Small amounts and actions matter because they accumulate.

The Wolf Parable

There is a parable that I like:
A grandfather is talking with his grandson, and he says there are two wolves inside of us, which are always at war with each other. One of them is a good wolf, which represents things like kindness, bravery, and love. The other is a bad wolf, which represents things like greed, hatred, and fear.

The grandson stops and thinks about it for a second; then, he looks up at his grandfather and says, "Grandfather, which one wins?"

The grandfather quietly replies, "The one you feed."

If you're always feeding debt, your debt will get bigger. Your mind will be clouded. You'll be worried. You'll attract problems, and you'll feel like you're always fighting fires.

If you feed your savings, your savings will get bigger. It may not happen overnight, but your money and your mindset will attract money and opportunities. If you want to have a garden, you have to plant seeds. Money provides the seeds to set the garden of your life. After that, it's a simple process to map out how you will achieve your goals.

When setting financial goals, think about how much you need to save and for how long. Then, think about how you will accomplish that saving. For most people, this means putting a set amount aside each month, according to their pay schedule. This monthly amount is the difference between just having a dream and making your dream a reality.

"The best time to plant a tree was 20 years ago.
The second best time is now."
– Chinese Proverb

"We are what we repeatedly do.
Excellence, then, is not an act but a habit."
– Aristotle

Start. Be disciplined. Set a savings regime and stick to it. Success lies in doing productive acts more and more, and unproductive things less and less. Action becomes habit. A habit becomes a practice; and, over time, a practice will become wealth.

Pay Yourself First

You are important. You earn money. You have bills and obligations. You likely pay everyone else and have nothing left for you. Pay yourself first. Take the money from cash amounts and stick it in a jar. Transfer a portion of the money when it comes into your account to savings before you do anything else.

Establish a Savings Amount

Whenever my kids get money, I ask them how much they need to save. They put that amount in a separate bank. I established 10% of their earnings as the portion that gets saved. I do it myself. When money comes in, 10% moves to savings. If you do this, you will always have money.

Measure Success

I previously mentioned your ESCG™ Code sheet. The clarity that this one piece of paper can give is very powerful. It's your financial picture on one page. Do a spreadsheet to calculate your goals and the length of time required to achieve them. Check your finances online. Move money to a savings account and watch it grow. It's really satisfying when the balances are positive and getting bigger.

Have several goals. A short-term goal might be to pay off debt. A medium-term goal may be to save for a down payment on a house. Long-term goals typically include plans for retirement, paying off a home, or helping children with education.

You do need to address your finances to get an idea of what resources you have to work with to achieve your goals. There are many tools to use to calculate your expenses. Or you can set up a spreadsheet to calculate after-tax income and your monthly expenses. The difference will be your discretionary income or earnings.

Now, the hard part: the debt. Let's just consider consumer debt, like credit cards. How much of your discretionary funds go toward paying down on these debts? I will tell you this one thing. With current credit card rates at 20%, credit card debt will kill whatever financial plan or goals you have. Obviously, the first thing that needs to happen is that you get rid of consumer debt.

The Rule of 72 gives you an indication of the effect of compounding rates of return. If you divide 72 by the rate of interest, the number will be the years to double. So, at 7%, 72/7 will give you 10.3 years to double your money. At 10%, 72/10 will give you 7.2 years to double. Conversely, if you use the Rule of 72 and 20% on interest paid, then 72/20% is 3.6 years. The amount you spent doubled in about 3.6 years with minimum payments. That is why the minimum payment is set so low.

What can you do about debt? Find a low cost credit card balance transfer. Or transfer to a line of credit and cut your card while you are paying the debt off. I have also done something that I call a *fiscal fast*. I just don't shop unless it is necessary, like for milk or produce. Generally, I have food things stored. This helps me clear foodstuffs so they don't get too old.

I rebuilt myself with small amounts. I disciplined myself to transfer 10% of money I received. It didn't matter how I got the money. I based this on David Chilton's book, *The Wealthy Barber*. I started slowly with jars. When I would get to $500, I would start a new jar. Then I had multiple jars; and then I had lots of jars—and then I decided I better put the money in the bank. I find this discipline really satisfying. Any money that comes in, I transfer 10% first thing to savings.

I was sceptical of books like *The Secret*. I had been a financial planner—a professional, advising people on managing money. It seemed kind of foolish to believe that you just wish for things and they appear. When you're in a bad situation, it seems compelling. So, I tried creative visualization, prayers, and keeping my mind positive. Nothing happened for me until I cleared my debts and started my jars. Then it was like magic.

For good things to happen in your life, you need to have the knowledge and resources, and the will to act on them. People seem to think that the good things that happen have to be in the form of a cheque. Sometimes it will be something you were looking to buy, or an investment opportunity, or a chance to do something you wanted to do. Savings will give you the resources to act when those good things happen.

The Value of Time

One of the other areas overlooked in savings is time. It is a good idea to know what the value of your time is to determine if you're really saving money. If you're driving an hour and shopping an hour, then, if you add the value of two hours to your purchase, you may find that the cost savings is not justified. Conversely, you may find that having meals prepared and delivered is a cost savings—if you're pressed for time.

How do you calculate the value of your time? Many would use their earning or wage rate. You might put a premium on your spare time.

Other Costs

There are many things that go into a purchase, not just the cost of the goods. Many people swear by Costco, but you may need a car to get to Costco, so that is a cost. There's the convenience element as well. You could go to three different grocery stores to save the maximum, or pick the one that best suits your purposes and pay a little more for some of your items.

Purchasing Like a Professional

"Beware of little expenses. A small leak will sink a great ship."
– Benjamin Franklin

In business, there's a whole profession—or in larger companies, a department—dedicated to buying goods and services for the public and private sector. Procurement and purchasing are key corporate functions. Procurement involves the process of selecting vendors, establishing payment terms, strategic vetting, selection, the negotiation of contracts, and the actual purchasing of goods. What do purchasing professionals do? How can you purchase like a pro?

Ultimately, in purchasing for a company, there is more strategy and thought put into the process. There is much at stake for production, distribution, the brand, marketing, and customer service, as well as cost and accounting.

Setting the Goal

The lowest price is an obvious goal but not always the best objective. The lowest price often comes with lower quality. Getting the most value for your money, based on your criteria, is the best bet. There are many other criteria for making purchases, such as convenience, value of time, sustainability, fair trade, local origin, reducing carbon footprint or waste. It's important to establish what you value most in your purchases.

Setting Your Criteria

What are the most important things to you in your purchase? Write these down. It's easy to have someone take you off track of what you want if you are dealing with a salesperson.

Research

It's easy to do some research online before purchasing. There are many ways to compare the same product with different retailers on a website like Amazon or Newegg. When you buy online, your main criteria is price, as it's not experience or relationship, or customer service. Some people like the online shopping experience, and others just use it to do research.

Here's something that is often overlooked in research: measurement. If you're purchasing furniture, measure what you have before you go to store. That way, you know what fits and can be brought into the house. You can also look up your car measurements online and compare them to your proposed car. Evaluate the differences. It's an expensive mistake to buy something that won't fit in the house or garage.

Negotiate

You can always ask for something. I will always ask for a discount where I can. Some purchases are highly negotiable, like buying a car. If you do purchase a car, there are tools that can help you get higher discounts and better options. When purchasing services, you can ask for more. In dealing with salespeople, sometimes just being nice or funny can get you something extra. Always be fair. Don't expect someone to not make or to lose money.

Strategy

Have a plan or objective with respect to purchasing. That strategy might be a budget. Another strategy would be to use loyalty or promotion points. I have an ongoing strategy with Shoppers Drug Mart to get the maximum amount of points every month. I load my coupons, decide the amount I need to spend, and spend that amount. I use my phone calculator to set my limit. I buy food there if it's the same price as the grocery store. There are people that do extreme couponing. Have a strategy. Plan, process, and execute.

Paying for Goods

I do purchase with credit. I purchase using my credit card for points and then pay off monthly. I have $4 bank accounts that give 12 transactions, and I minimize the transactions by using the credit card.
If you aren't disciplined with credit, leave the cards alone. If you use cash, you have a limit. You can use your smart phone calculator to add as you shop.

Measuring Results

There are good software tools for tracking expenses and purchases. Evaluating your spending can help keep you on track.

The Impulse Buy and How to Avoid It

As you track your money and spending, you may discover that some of your money gets used for things you don't need. Impulse spending is unplanned spending, purchasing things that you may or may not need, or spending more on an item than you'd like to.

Learn to separate recreational trips and buying trips. Instead of recreational shopping, go for a walk in nature, which is better for your health. If you still want to shop, go to a thrift store for a treasure hunt— buy things that you love rather than because they're cheap. Leave your debit and credit cards at home. Use cash, as it sets limits, and you'll be more careful with limits.

People spend impulsively for a variety of reasons. If you are in a good mood, you may spend out of pleasure and to keep the good mood. If you are in a bad mood, you spend to make yourself feel better. Impulse spending habits are often linked to stress levels. A little stress can be motivating, but a lot of stress can impair your ability to make wise choices. You need to address short-term thinking because a purchase may create a long-term debt. Debt is just more stress. Keep yourself in a better frame of mind, and you can stop impulse buying.

Guilt is another emotion that makes people spend. You may have been lead to believe that love comes from the mall. Gifts are a measure of love. If guilt is your problem, then consider alternatives: giving of time; giving of home-made items; giving of thrift finds; sharing a meal. Learn to set limits. Tell people what your limits are. You'll be surprised how accommodating your friends and family can be.

When people receive things they don't want or need, it can be stressful. Some people are minimalist, so buying them knickknacks just serves to annoy them. I find buying consumables is a safe and affordable gift.

Impulse buying may also be situational. You may spend in certain places or times because you feel obligated to do so, such as on vacation, during holiday seasons, when you're with certain people or while engaging in specific activities. If you've set your goals, then you'll have the focus and discipline to set priorities and to address these circumstances. Stick a picture of one of your goals on your fridge or mirror to help you stay focused.

Set Priorities

There's a cliché that the key to good money management is separating needs from wants. Unless something is necessary for survival, it's a want. I believe the key is setting priorities. When your priority is to stick to your budget, then your spending will be managed. If you aren't sure if an item is important, do without it for a period of time.

Put some effort into financials for essentials like shelter or transportation. For instance, you may have evaluated all possible transportation methods for you to get to work, and decided that you need to purchase a car. Fine, but which car you buy is another choice you make.

Do you buy the more expensive SUV that you want, or will a more economical vehicle meet your needs? Almost everything you buy involves a want vs. need determination; and, ultimately, how you make these choices will determine if you reach your goals or not.

I'll give you some shopping suggestions for clothes, food, and car purchases. I can provide you with other programs or savings ideas, if you would like to subscribe to **goals@thesmart moneyguide.com**.

> *"By failing to prepare, you are preparing to fail."*
> – Benjamin Franklin

> *"A simple fact that is hard to learn is that*
> *the time to save money is when you have some."*
> – Joe Moore

The art and mindset of savings may seem trite. If you want to drive a race car, you still need to know how to park. The same applies to the multiple skills necessary in money management: making money, saving money, investing money, and giving money. All skills are important.

What aspect of savings is most important to you?

What is the most important thing you learned here about purchasing?

Saving:
Goal # 1: Eliminate credit debt
Goal # 2: Save 10%
Goal # 3: Save 3 months living expenses
Goal # 4 _____

Words to look up:

Chapter Eight

Creating

"In the beginning, God created the heavens and the earth."
(Genesis 1:1)

"The creation of a thousand forests is in one acorn."
– Ralph Waldo Emerson

*"The way to activate the seeds of your creation is by
making choices about the results you want to create.
When you make a choice, you activate vast human energies and
resources, which otherwise go untapped."*
– Robert Fritz

Wealth and Health

You are interested in creating wealth. You may have come to assume that wealth is based in money. The origin of the word is from Middle English *welthe*, from well or *weal*, on the pattern of health. You should always have health as a priority, but you may forget and measure wealth in terms of money. Health is another asset, and you should always make it a priority. In creating wealth, you are in turn creating health – the ability to enjoy life.

Opportunity, Knowledge, Resources, and Action

In the *Savings* chapter, I discussed having the resources to act when good things come into your life. In this section, I'll refer to creating wealth, which is another way of having money working for you. Essentially, in creating wealth, you are leveraging your time and money.

Opportunity is the start of creating wealth. There are three parts to opportunity.

Knowledge is recognizing the opportunity. You have to be aware and have the knowledge of a topic to realize a good deal, whether that's in real estate, business, or securities. If I said this building is at a 10% cap rate, or this mining company found two ounces of gold per tonne in their core samples, would you know if this is a good deal? If you're looking to build wealth in a certain area, building your knowledge is possible at any income level or net worth. You can work on your knowledge while you are saving.

Resources – Often, you need some money to do things, invest, or participate. You may be able to participate by arranging a deal for investors, but I've generally found that investors want to see some of your money aligned with theirs. This is why you need savings. Opportunities often need action, and by the time you get investors, or move money around, it's gone.

> *"Opportunity is missed by most people*
> *because it is dressed in overalls and looks like work."*
> – Thomas Edison

> *"If opportunity doesn't knock, build a door."*
> – Milton Berle

> *"When it's raining gold, put out the bucket not the thimble."*
> – Warren Buffett

Action – To realize an opportunity, you need to act. Opportunities are continually presented, but not all are acted on. To act isn't always easy. Often, it involves overcoming inertia or fear. You can look at deals all day long, but you can't make money looking at deals without acting. You can improve your decision-making and ability to act by developing or using systems. You can build more wealth by acting more frequently. This seems simple, but most people fail to act on opportunity. They get overwhelmed by potential problems. In acting, you put yourself in motion. You may encounter the problems; but, in action, you can also set your mind to finding solutions.

"The most difficult thing is the decision to act; the rest is merely tenacity. The fears are paper tigers. You can do anything you decide to do. You can act to change and control your life; and the procedure, the process, is its own reward."
– Amelia Earhart

"You miss 100% of the shots you never take."
– Wayne Gretzky

What Makes a Successful Investor?

First, there are many different definitions of success. Return is only one. I will describe different aspects of investing that will make you a successful investor.

Discipline

One of the most important factors in successful investing is discipline. Most people don't realize what the real difference is between an individual investor (called a retail investor by the investment industry) and a professional or institutional investor. You may think that it's the amount of money involved in the deal, or a certain account size. Knowledge—the highest level is called *sophisticated*. This is a characteristic of institutional investors, but regular investors can be sophisticated too. The main difference is discipline. Professional investors set a method or mandate, or recipe, and they stick to it. Their recipe will be different between funds or managers, but they will all be disciplined.

Knowledge

"Formal education will make you a living;
self-education will make you a fortune."
– Jim Rohn

"If money is your hope for independence, you will never have it. The only real security that a man will have in this world is a reserve of knowledge, experience, and ability."
– Henry Ford

One of the key criteria in what you can invest in is your knowledge. The investment industry is required to categorize you based on what they perceive your knowledge is. You shouldn't invest in things you don't understand.

Knowledge is something you can affect. You don't have to acquire your securities or realtors license to become knowledgeable in these investments. Some of the best investors I've known have been individuals who have a keen interest in an area. I taught myself real estate financials to see what real estate investors were getting as returns. I specialized in high yield and REITs (Real Estate Income Trusts).

Some sophisticated investors still use advisors. There's some value in speaking to someone about investing to get a different perspective. Even when you are at a high level in skill and knowledge, you don't have all the answers. Nobody does. Having a sounding board can help make better decisions.

If you're looking for an advisor, it's my suggestion that you look for someone who presents like a coach. You're looking for someone who supports your goals, understands where you are coming from, takes the time to know you, and has some investment insights that complement yours. They might not be exactly the same, but you'll get better decisions out of dialogue. Essentially, with an advisor, you should invest with less risk, and structure your portfolio to protect your assets.

Methodology

There are 10,000+ publicly traded companies in the US. In Canada there are 1400+ small cap junior mining stocks. Real Estate Income Trusts (REITs). Exchange Traded Funds (ETFs). Thousands of mutual funds.

This is where the confusion starts. There are so many choices. You may think someone else is picking all the right ones. First, come from certainty, not confusion. Have a methodology of how you pick stocks. Understand what you are buying. If you are buying a stock, you are buying a business. With diversified investments, like mutual funds, you are buying management.

What is a methodology? Methodology: 1) a body of methods, rules, and postulates employed by a discipline; a particular procedure or set of procedures; 2) the analysis of the principles or procedures of inquiry in a particular field. In investing, methodology is a way of setting your criteria for selecting investments. You might pick based on professional research, price to earnings ratio, sector or diversification, dividend yield, moving averages. Once you set criteria, it is much easier to make choices because your criteria eliminate what you don't want and focuses you on what you do want.

Warren Buffet did not become the world's greatest investor by picking stocks, but by developing a very effective methodology for picking stocks. He has a formula for calculating share value and he evaluated the business, brand and financial performance of the companies he considered for investment.

My methodology was clear. My stock selection was set by the firm. I could only recommend analyst covered stocks. That eliminated many lesser quality securities. I focussed on high yield dividend paying stocks. Then I used moving averages; buying below the moving average as the stock would eventually return to the mean. My methodology gave above average returns with less than market risk.

Real estate investors may also develop and use a methodology for investing. They may use capitalization rates for selecting distressed or income properties, or a formula for assessing properties for flipping.

Building wealth is not so much about winning the game, but playing the game. Too much emphasis about investment are about stock picking and setting a very difficult goal – the highest return. Establish a methodology and set your goals and your course of action will become clear.

Developing an investment methodology is the first step in a creating wealth strategy. An investment methodology involves more than picking stocks or properties. Investing involves reviewing the portfolio, realigning positions, asset allocation and selling. In real estate it also includes management and maintenance plans.

Managing Emotions

> *"There is a sufficiency in the world for man's need*
> *but not for man's greed."*
> – Mahatma Gandhi

Managing investments is to a great extent, managing emotions. The cycle of emotion in markets is well documented, so it's worth understanding. The first part of the cycle begins with optimism. The market sentiment is positive. You expect things to go your way. You expect a return for the risk of investing.

As expectations are met, it is common for you to get excited about the possibility of even greater returns. The excitement becomes thrilling as returns exceed your expectations. At the top of the cycle is when you experience thrill and euphoria. It's at this point where you're at the point of maximum financial risk. You stop seeing risk and see only potential. You think you're brilliant. You can beat the market. High returns are yours for the taking, and you can tolerate higher levels of risk.

The second phase of the cycle happens when the market stops meeting your expectations and begins to turn. At first, you watch the market for signs of direction. Anxiety turns to denial and then to fear, as the value of investments decline. Many people will then start to act defensively and may think about switching out of riskier assets to more defensive asset classes. Other emotions in this stage are complacency, denial, and hope.

In the third phase of the cycle, the realities of a bear market become apparent, and you may become desperate. You may panic and withdraw from the market altogether—afraid of further losses. If you continue, you may wonder whether the market is going to recover and whether you should be in the market at all. The emotions of this stage are panic, capitulation, and despondency. Ironically, you will commonly fail to recognize you're actually at the point of maximum financial opportunity. *Smart Money* recognizes this opportunity and the emotions of panicked investors.

In the fourth stage of the cycle, you may experience skepticism as to when the markets will recover. You may feel caution or worry, wondering if market growth will return, and you may be reluctant to invest money in the market at this point, even though prices are relatively low and opportunities are attractive. The emotions of this stage are doubt, skepticism, caution, and worry.

What does *Smart Money* make of emotions? Irrational investors create opportunities for rational investors. You just have to manage your negative emotions. Just as in the early stage, you have to have discipline to manage the positive emotions. It is important to remember that markets change, and investments go in and out of favour. Emotions exacerbate markets and returns. The following are the five most common emotional-based situations that create problems for investors ...

Overconfidence – You over-rate your ability to pick investments or sectors.

Loss aversion – A loss causes about twice as much pain as a gain causes pleasure. During periods of market volatility, you will likely experience the sense of loss more acutely.

Chasing Past Performance – You focus on the past, or on investments that became long-term holds, rather than look to the future.

Timing the Market – Even the best investors can't reliably predict the market's movements in the short term.

Managing Risk – Institutional investors have discipline to take profits and sell winning and losing investments to keep their portfolio allocation. How would I describe institutional investors? Institutional investors are playing chess when everyone else is playing checkers. They have a longer time horizon and are using strategy and discipline. Your average retail investor is often just reacting.

Greed and Fear

> *"Greed is normally balanced by fear."*
> – Peter Schiff

Greed is an emotion worth understanding. Some will say greed is the highest form of motivation. If you think about it, greed, hatred, envy, and jealousy are negative emotions.

Greed is an excessive love of money, profit, possession, or consumption. The operative word is excessive. There is nothing wrong with the creation of wealth. There is a problem when it is at the expense of something or everything else.

What does greed produce? Greed produces corruption. It produces profit at the expense of the environment, health, and safety. It creates unsustainable and exploitative business relationships and practices. It creates management and worker discord. Greed produces bubbles and losses.

To be a good investor, you really need to understand and manage greed. How do you manage greed? Consider character and discipline. Understand that greed and loss can go hand in hand. Generally, with higher returns, the risks are higher. Understand other stakeholders and their contribution to success.

Fear is the most powerful emotional motivator. Fear messages are generally far more effective than pleasure messages. Marketers, politicians, and the media create and manipulate fear. Fear of loss keeps greed in check. Creating fear on its own is not a good strategy or motivator. People shut down, make mistakes, or become unpredictable when they are stressed by too much fear.

"Courage is resistance to fear, mastery of fear, not absence of fear."
– Mark Twain

Managing Risk

A key function that's overlooked by most non-professional investors is risk management. You may be more interested in the making money function rather than the protecting money function. The making of money is the *Coco Puffs*, and the managing risk part is the *Wheat Bran* of investing. Making money is fun and exciting, and managing risk is boring but good for you. You can't have a steady diet of fun and excitement, without consequences. Keep perspective. Risk management is often more a function of experience than academic learning. You can benefit from someone else's experience through a mentor or advisor's experience because everyone makes mistakes, and someone with experience has paid their dues.

"Rule No. 1: Never lose money. Rule No. 2: Never forget rule No. 1."
– Warren Buffett

Investment Goals and Risk Management

For many, the obvious goal is the highest return. High return often comes with high risk, and with higher risk, sometimes you get no or negative return. You can always look back in perfect hindsight, but that is not what investing is. Investing is making calculated risks for calculated returns.

Risk Adjusted Returns

Most people are familiar with rates of return on investments. I'd like you to consider risk adjusted rates of return. *Risk adjusted* means that if two investments have the same rate of return— let's say 10%—then the better investment is the one with less risk.

In my experience, the best people to qualify and quantify risk are those professionally trained to do so. That means the securities industry. It doesn't mean that they don't get it wrong; they just get it wrong less often. The securities market provides the easiest way of diversifying, which is a way of mitigating risk.

Real estate investing is one of the better risk adjusted returns, but that being said, real estate investing is not without risk. It is also not without work.

Sophisticated Investor

You may have heard this term. It is a judgement or qualitative description used by the investment industry to categorize a type of investor. What makes an investor a *sophisticated* investor? For investment dealers, it is knowledge and experience. Knowledge is based on an interview of the investor with an advisor. Experience—what has the investor invested in previously? Individual stocks, in high concentration; options; commodities; or short strategies are the hallmarks of a sophisticated investor.

How I look at an individual's knowledge is based on the levels or dimensions they understand. Most people understand the dynamics of supply and demand: low supply, high demand, the value goes up, and vice versa. This is two dimensions.

Sometimes two dimensions, or supply and demand, are not the whole story. Take the value of oil, for example. At one point, the price of oil went up, and you might think it was because demand increased, but it was mainly due to the value of the USD falling. In this case, there are three dimensions: supply, demand, and the value of the USD.

Another dimension might be interest rates. The reason the USD fell was because the US government lowered interest rates. Supply, demand, USD, interest rates: four dimensions. Maybe there was an event, like 9/11 or a financial crisis. Supply, demand, USD, interest rates, and event: five dimensions. You might add technical or quantitative analysis. That is looking at moving averages, charts, or formations to predict outcomes: six dimensions.

Your average retail investor understands two dimensions: supply and demand. A sophisticated investor understands 3 or more. Are there more dimensions than what I have mentioned? Absolutely. This is where hedge fund managers operate—derivatives, technical analysis, quantitative analysis, big data, artificial intelligence, and machine learning. There are more I haven't listed.

Hedge funds can have more strategies than these. Generally, you need to be either a sophisticated or an accredited investor to invest in a hedge fund. How do you get to these levels? First, you need to be aware that there are more levels than supply and demand. When you read, or watch the news, read between the lines. Do more due diligence and research. This is how hedge funds make their returns. They use more information to make investment decisions.

What is the benefit of being a sophisticated investor? You have to be sophisticated before an investment dealer will allow you to invest in certain products. You shouldn't invest in things that you don't understand. Part of the role of an investment advisor is to prevent you from getting into products you don't understand.

Accredited Investor

An accredited investor is one with a certain net worth and income level, as defined by the investment industry regulators. Investments that are private or higher risk may require you to be an accredited investor.

Indicators

Indicators are statistics, indexes or references that institutional or sophisticated investors use to forecast the trend of a market. Understanding the trend helps you position investments to your advantage. Economic indicators such as employment rates, the trade balance, and inflation give an indication as to the health and direction of the economy. The Case-Shiller index provides data on house prices. Other real estate indicators are new housing starts or foreclosures.

In the stock market, there is often great discussion of the most common stock indexes. IPOs are also an indication of the health of the market. More IPOs indicate a more positive market.

Many investors also use technical analysis to enhance their decision-making. Moving averages, MACD (moving average convergence divergence) and relative strength are very accessible tools for retail investors. Another chart I found helpful is Point and Figure. Before computers, stock brokers used to use box graph paper and charted trends daily by hand. It is still a very accurate tool to predict direction and targets.

What if the indicators are negative? Professional investors make money in up and down markets. Some of the biggest wins were made by hedge fund managers that read the indicators and profited from market collapses. Just position yourself to take advantage of a downturn.

Market Volatility

In the stock market, it is entirely possible that the market will go down 25%. It is also entirely possible that that downturn will be recovered in days, weeks, months or years. How do you deal with market volatility? How do you not panic when the market drops 25% over a day or three days?   Just stop yourself and ask yourself, "Were prices lower ten years ago?" Will prices be higher or lower ten years from now?" You can't predict very accurately in the short term what is going to happen, but over the longer term it is easier. Set your sights out further in time.

Value Investing

Value investing is a discipline of investing in companies with earnings and dividend paying stocks. When you compare to other types of investing, this category provides better risk adjusted returns. Growth may outperform but with higher risk. For most people who are investing saved or earned monies, buying dividend paying stocks is the way to go.

Growth Investing

Growth investing is investing in companies based on potential. Valuation is based on projections of future revenue. A growth investment may have no or negative earnings, and the valuation is based on the potential of the company.

Probability and Quartile

I suggest you think in terms of probability of success. Generally, when presented with a scenario, I mentally calculate a probability, with investments and with people. With an investment, you should have an expected return and expected probability of getting that return. This is just for illustration. For example, you might expect a 9% return with an 80% chance of success. In this illustration, you might reasonably expect a return of 9% x .8 = 7.2%. Over the longer term, then, you might expect this return: 80% probability that you will get 9%, but a 20% chance of nothing, lower or negative. If you are presented with a projected 100% return, what is the probability of success?

The investment industry measures success in investment in terms of quartiles: first, second, third, and fourth or bottom quartile. Obviously, you want to be in the first, above average return quartile. Second is good. Third is okay, with room for improvement. Fourth? No one wants to be bottom quartile.

When people present to you, keep probability in mind. You can also apply probability to people. Does a person do what he says he is going to? When you come across someone who is more unlikely to do what he said he was going to do, than likely, what do you think? Think of quartiles: top quartile, 2nd quartile, 3rd quartile, and bottom quartile. People who do what they say they are going to do and achieve more than expected? Top quartile. People who do what they say and perform above expected? Second quartile. At expectations. Bottom quartile? People who overstate and underperform. They never do what they say they are going to do.

Correlation and Cause

Understand the difference between correlation and cause. Correlation means that there is a relationship between two things. Cause means, something affects something. There are opportunities or better understanding of risk if you understand the relationship between things. For example, the price of oil and the Canadian dollar has a positive correlation, meaning a movement in the price of oil generally has a similar movement in the value of the Canadian dollar. You might see the price of oil increasing, so you might assume the demand for oil is increasing and it is a good buying opportunity. Supply and demand have a causal relationship to the price of oil. I would suggest you look at the USD index and see if the USD is falling because of correlation: the price of oil to go up as contracting parties in oil have currency conversions; so they pay more in USD because the dollar has fallen relative to other currencies.

Often, people perceive that relationships are causal, when they are correlated. Causal means that something causes a change in the other. Just because two things are correlated, it does not necessarily mean that there is a causal relationship. There is a tendency in the media and the public to construe causal relationships, to blame or paint a negative picture. It's much better for you to understand how things really relate to each other.

Endowment Effect

Have you seen someone ask a ridiculous price for something or refuse to sell for a reasonable price? The *Endowment Effect* is a hypothesis put forward by psychologist, Jean Piaget, who observed that children quickly developed a notion of ownership. Based on observation and experiments, he established the Endowment Effect Theory, which suggests people tend to overvalue things that they own.

When you want to buy or sell a collectible, property, or investment, be aware of this psychological bias. If you're negotiating with someone, this may help you understand where someone is coming from and work through irrationality with reason.

In investments, you may see the importance of this. When you own a property, collectible, or security, to a certain degree, you lose objectivity. This is one of the reasons that the investment industry is very careful about the investment choices of advisors and analysts when it comes to making recommendations. This is another reason that it might be worthwhile to have an independent advisor guide you in negotiating a sale. You may simply have unrealistic expectations about the value of your property or asset and an advisor can help you determine a fair market value to sell in a reasonable time period.

Understanding this bias might also help you recognize a bubble. Robert Shiller coined the phrase, *irrational exuberance.* If an investment is largely promoted by people who own it, then it has one of the characteristics of a bubble. *"Never ask a barber if you need a haircut."* If someone is recommending something, consider if their bias is more than just a commission.

Investing versus Speculation

spec·u·la·tion *noun*

1) the forming of a theory or conjecture without firm evidence. 2) investment in stocks, property, or other ventures in the hope of gain but with the risk of loss.

Investing and speculation are very similar, with the difference being speculation is based on assumptions or a hypothesis. The speculative investment is riskier because of the lack of proof or verified results. Results like production yield, drug efficacy or customer adoption may be projected.

There is a phrase, *"bleeding edge"*. This refers to early investors taking a hit by investing based on flawed assumptions. In early technology investing, the company management is often still researching and testing and sometimes their assumptions don't work to plan. It is not intent to mislead, but when you go into uncharted territory, the only way to proceed is to establish some assumptions. This is why there is a great deal of attention on results – to see how accurate management's assumptions were.

Speculative investments often crop up after something is hugely successful. After Facebook, you had many social media companies follow suit. Then, medical marijuana and digital currencies. First, these types of investments should only be in your high risk category. No one puts their whole net worth on a high risk bet.

Now, are these investments of merit? These are the types of investments where you can make a great deal of money, or you can lose it all. There are professional speculators. They put a great deal of time and effort into their selections and often have the benefit of diversification. For your average investor, the odds are against speculation working out. You will have newsletter writers and others touting past history. The problem with these is that all the risks are known. Everything worked out. They aren't going to advertise what didn't work out.

How do you know something is too risky? When people stop seeing risk. That's the riskiest stage. What can you do in a speculative market? *Smart Money* is usually in early and takes profit. If you are in a speculative market, sell enough to take your initial investment out, and let the rest ride. Another way of mitigating risk is using moving averages. *Smart Money* knows that markets go back to the mean. Professional investors have a selling discipline to limit exposure.

"Gambling: The sure way of getting nothing for something."
– Wilson Mizner

Gambling is beyond speculation. There are professional gamblers who do make money. For the most part, gambling should be just considered entertainment. That's if you find losing money entertaining.

Hedging

Hedging is literally from the word hedge – a protective border. In other words, hedging is putting a limit on risk. Hedging is a strategy used by an investor or company management to protect a position against adverse conditions, like price or demand changes. A company producing oil, might hedge to cover its production costs. It might buy a contract to sell its oil to a speculator for $50, so if the price drops below to $45, the hedger sells at $50 and the speculator gets a loss. If the price of oil goes to $55, then the hedger sells at $50 and the speculator makes $5.

Hedge funds originally hedged against adverse market conditions to make money in up and down markets and limit risk using derivatives. You can do this with options on stock indexes.

Hedge funds can use short strategies – selling investments they don't own, with the intent that if the investment goes down, they can buy it back at a lower price than they sold it for a profit. You are likely familiar with a long strategy – buy low, sell high. Short is sell high, buy low, when you expect something to go down in value.

Hedge funds can use leverage – which is borrowing to invest. This can enhance returns, if you can borrow at 4% and get a return of 9%, you can earn an additional 5%. This can also work against the hedge fund if the leveraged investment is a loss.

Hedge funds can use derivatives which are contracts or options to hold a position for a period of time. Usually the contract allows you to buy or sell a position. The contract cost or premium is low relative to the position value.

These strategies have the potential to provide higher returns, but at the same time, create greater losses and in some cases greater than the money invested. That is why they aren't available to the general investing community. Hedge funds have fewer restrictions than do regular mutual funds or exchange traded funds have.

Trading versus Investing

With software tools, day or high frequency trading has been promoted. Investing is a longer-term pursuit, with some analysis or due diligence. Trading is speculative: buying something based on market trend and technical analysis rather than assessment of the underlying security. If you decide to go this route, start with a small amount. There is more to day trading than you might think. The emotional component is a key determinant of success. Some will simply find trading too stressful.

Bubbles

Why do bubbles happen? I have observed numerous bubbles over the years: BreX and mining, Dotcom and technology, Beanie Babies, real estate, and the latest in digital currencies. Bubbles may start out as plausible investments, but the valuation gets out of hand. Bubbles and speculation happen because of greed and unrealistic expectations. People simply set aside prudence for the prospect of high returns. The psychology of speculation and bubbles is very well documented. Irrational behaviour is actually very predictably irrational. When the speculative market runs out of willing investors, or some other market event, bubbles burst. You might make money and be on the right side of the transaction, and you might not. In euphoria, you can't tell someone that something is too risky. More often, in speculation, people hold on too long because the projections keep going up, and they don't want to give up return.

When you look at past bubbles, like dotcom companies or US real estate, there were real companies or assets that had a valuation matrix. When valuating companies, it is *price to earnings* ratios. Real estate has cap rate, and build or replacement cost. In both cases, the value of the assets rose above the generally held valuation methods to unsustainable levels. With real estate, the leverage levels became unsustainable based on value.

How can you identify bubbles? If there's discussion in the media whether something is a bubble, chances are it's a bubble. Look at the valuation. Does it make sense, or is emphasis placed on a future valuation? If the emphasis is on the future value, chances are it's a bubble. Who's promoting it as an investment? If it's by people who own it that have drank the Kool-Aid, chances are it's a bubble.

Can you make money in bubbles? Yes, but understand it is speculative and risky. What investors misunderstand and miscalculate is the downside. When a speculative market breaks, the downside from selling pressure is fast and furious. *Smart Money* often sees the bubble forming and prepares to make money on the downside. The selling pressure can bring down in days what took months to rise. The selling pressure is always greater than the buying pressure.

The people who recognize a bubble breaking early are the ones who make money. They're watching for signs of the bubble breaking. The others who make money on bubbles take the contrarian view, and they short the market. You can do this with *put options*. Puts are options to sell something at a given price. You buy something at one price and a put allows you to sell it at a higher price.

Black Swans

A Black Swan is an unpredictable or unforeseen event with extreme consequences. Examples of black swan events are 9/11 or the Japanese tsunami. The negative event puts disruption or sometimes panic into a market. The effect of the event is bad, but the reaction to the event is worse.

Financial plans can be jeopardized if you are guided by emotions. This is where the role of the financial advisor can help you separate your emotions from reality and steer you on the path of rational investing. You can avoid the emotional roller coaster by being aware of the emotions you are likely to experience.

Costs of Securities Investing

There are costs involved with investing. In securities, if you do go through a financial advisor and have the resources, choose a fee based advisor. The fees are tax deductible. You can also achieve lower per transaction costs and make decisions based on merit. Some people do not buy or sell securities, simply because they can't get their head around paying commissions to make money or take a loss. With a fee based account, you set your fees based on assets, not transactions.

If you wish to have lower costs on your returns, then look towards passive investments. Passive investments look to manage returns against a benchmark, and minimize trading. Typically, these are Exchange Traded Funds (ETFs) or Index Based Funds. You don't need an advisor as much here because the fund company differences are marginal. It is just a matter of asset allocation.

If you wish to focus on return, then you're looking for active management. There are higher costs involved as there is more research, trading, and intellectual property involved.

There are times when active management is going to outperform passive index investing. Sideways markets (where the market is flat for a longer period) favours active management. If markets trend upwards, the case for indexing and passive investing is stronger.

Taxes

Another consideration is taxes. Managing your investments tax efficiently; trading effectively (not overtrading and tax loss selling); and sheltering growth in registered accounts— this is where having an investment advisor working with your accountant helps. There are advisors who have more expertise in tax and accounting issues. Again, if you use a fee based advisor, the fees are tax deductible.

Taxes are a cost of investing, and many people look at paying taxes as a bad thing. Paying taxes means you made money. That money is going to infrastructure to help you make more money. It is going for healthcare, education, power and transportation infrastructure, or justice. These are all things that contribute to your wealth and capacity to increase wealth.

Management Team

Remember, in all investments, you are investing in people. Pay close attention to the management team. There is not one great idea or resource asset that can survive faulty execution and execution is through people. Carefully evaluate the team and their track record.

Teamwork is not as easy as you might think. It's one of those things you might overlook, but how does one team work well together while others flounder? A team is a product and the result of management. Dysfunctional management will produce a dysfunctional team. Confusion, poor risk management, mixed messages, or bullying will produce a poor team.

"Teamwork is the ability to work together toward a common vision. The ability to direct individual accomplishments toward organizational objectives. It is the fuel that allows common people to attain uncommon results."
– Andrew Carnegie

I have worked with productive and unproductive teams, and I must say unproductive is painful. It's difficult for even a high functioning person to perform and thrive under dysfunctional mismanagement. Business is the results of a team; and a management team that can cultivate a great team, which combines creativity, individual responsibility and contribution, and communicates well, will offer much better returns.

Control

One of the key considerations in investing is control of your money. Investing in securities is very clear—you own and direct your investments. When investing in private deals or partnerships, then control of your money is an issue. Often, private investing transfers control to management. Consider the competence and background of the management team and whether you are comfortable giving them control of your money.

Liquidity

This is another word for how easy it is to sell or liquidate your investment. When entering a private deal, have a clear idea as to the time frame involved and how you will realize your return.

Leverage

Leverage is another way of saying *borrowing to invest*. A mortgage is a form of leverage. Margin is another. Margin is the securities industries word for borrowing. Margin is automatically granted based on the nature of the stocks or securities, not the credit worthiness of the investor.

Leverage works when the growth of assets is higher than the borrowing rate. Unfortunately, this is not always the case: leverage in real estate. The banks are the gatekeeper and will typically not lend to you if you are over extended. The financial crisis of 2008 was largely a crisis of excess leverage and poor lending practices by major financial institutions.

Concentration versus Diversification

Wealthy people often build wealth through concentration. Business owners do it through building their own business. Others build by their profession—building a practice. It can also be done through specific industry sectors, like oil and gas, mining, media or real estate. Most of these strategies are based on specialized knowledge and investment of time and capital in a singular pursuit. People who are highly tied to one sector may diversify, even though concentration is their key wealth creation tool.

Many people are salaried, and their income is tied to one source. In such cases, your investment choices are in securities, and you should want to have your securities investments to be diversified. The rationale in the public markets is that projected returns in different sectors are not known. For all the research and analysis, the stock market remains somewhat of a mystery to even its experts. Diversification is a risk management tool. Most people will not make their fortunes in the stock market. Their investment portfolio will be from sales of assets, earnings or savings, and capital preservation, and modest growth will be their key goals.

> *"If you want more money, don't pay attention to the money. Pay attention to the thing that makes the money."*
> – Brandon Steiner

Negotiation

Negotiate: verb; 1) obtain or bring about by discussion. 2) find a way over or through (an obstacle or difficult path). 3) transfer (a check, bill, or other document) to the legal ownership of another person. 4) convert (a check) into cash. Origin early 17th century: from Latin *negotiat-* 'done in the course of business,' from the verb *negotiari, from negotium* 'business,' from *neg- 'not' + otium* 'leisure.'

Negotiation is a skill that is key to creating wealth. How to negotiate well? Negotiations will go better if you think about creating a value proposition for both sides. Many will only focus on what is in it for them. A great negotiation is where both sides come away thinking they got a good deal. If you think about what is in it for the other side, and articulate it to them, then you are on your way to being a better than average negotiator.

Understand what is important to you and the other party. There are generally three parts to a value proposition - risk/return, time frame and liquidity event. Promoters often think that the most important thing is the return, but that is not the case. The time frame and liquidity can be just as important to the investor. There are other factors that might contribute to a negotiation, such as synergies in business. If you are a good negotiator, more opportunities will come to you by reputation.

Personal Values, Sustainability, and Ethics

There are several approaches to investing by personal values. You can invest as an activist investor to affect the policies and behaviours of companies or industries from within. Usually, this is only effective if you own a substantial block or can be a director, but sometimes an activist investor might ask for your proxy, which is another way of asking if they can vote for you.

The other way is to invest in companies that have strong governance. They may articulate that they consider a triple bottom line—financial, environmental, and social. They may have strong operating policies coupled with ethics. This helps them do better by avoiding problems, risk, and lawsuits.

The third way is to invest directly in what you would like to see more of—like solar projects or renewable energy—or avoid certain sectors, such as gambling, defence, alcohol, fossil fuels, etc. For example, some investors have divested or sold investments in fossil fuels. There's a growing interest in socially responsible investing, and there are indications that the returns are slightly better. Investing for the good does well in returns.

Triple Bottom Line

You might think, in investing, that the only thing that matters is profit and earnings. A triple bottom line approach evaluates business or investment, based on societal, environmental, and financial considerations. What does that mean? It means that the business or investment provides a societal good or benefit, minimizes damage, or enhances the environment, and creates profit. In this respect, a triple bottom line opportunity is more likely to succeed because it has more legs to success. If you think that profit at the expense of something else is a good thing, consider that this is very short-term thinking.

We live on a planet, and we are all connected. So, if an opportunity provides profit—let's use a mine as an example: it produces ore and tailings, and a liability. It produces health damages. You have profit, but possibly lawsuits, and bad will. The same project, using new remediation technology, restores the environment, improves health, and provides well-paying employment opportunities. You have profit and a clean environment, which fosters health, business development in the community, and goodwill.

The first option is short-term thinking—based on a quarter or share price. The latter is more focused on the long term and sustainability. Again, evaluate returns over time. The latter should have the same or better return.

Stakeholders

It seems the only stakeholders that matter in investing are the investor and management. Public company management seems to be accountable only to shareholders. There are other stakeholders to consider: the work force (jobs), the country or community (economic benefit), customers (product), suppliers (business), the government (taxes), the environment, or future generations. Does the return to investor take precedence over the interests of other stakeholders?

In globalization and the pursuit of returns, management made changes to lower labour costs, and expected all other things to stay the same. So in the example of offshoring jobs or production, some people lost jobs domestically. Their jobs were costs and were not supposed to affect the revenue side. Labour is simply a cost. That's not what we saw. We've seen an increase in job insecurity. Job insecurity has had an impact on society.

On the other side, where labour costs are low, did we see the jobs created lead to sustainable employment? In some cases, it did, but in others, it seems to just be corporate exploitation in below standard of living wages. The international labour market system will never work if people are forced to compete against people working to death. If you can tell me that price is all that matters, then we only have to look at the outcome: civil unrest; the movement of refugees from areas of exploitation to areas of lower exploitation. Simply bring balance to the system. The cost is being born, just not by the corporations. It is the cost of misery. If we can look back at slavery and see how wrong it was, how is profiting from people working to death any better?

I am going to give a definition of a sustainable and fair job: It's one that provides ESCG™, the ability to earn a fair living, to be able have some savings, to be able to create wealth, and to give.

Now, given two opportunities, would it be better to have investor interests and other stakeholder relationships aligned? *Smart Money* is about being aware. The more stakeholders are in alignment, the better the predictability of positive outcome. Be aware in the choices you make. Consider the other stakeholders and whether there are good relationships and alignment of interests. Where there's more alignment, there's less risky returns.

> *"Where globalization means, as it so often does, that the rich and powerful now have new means to further enrich and empower themselves at the cost of the poorer and weaker, we have a responsibility to protest in the name of universal freedom."*
> – Nelson Mandela

Rate of Return and Time

Generally, we think in per annum returns. If a mortgage is posted at 4.2%, it is generally accepted as being 4.2% per year. This may seem obvious, but often what people overlook is the time period to get the return. One hundred percent rate of return in one year is great. But what if 100% rate of return over 10 years is 7 % per year? Just be careful how the rate of return is presented to you, because these little tricks are used.

Promoters often post past returns. If you bought this stock at this time (IPO or when recommended) and held to such and such date, you would have achieved this great return. The time line may have been given, but the return is not presented in a per annum rate. The annual return can be calculated but it is still a bit misleading and designed to appeal to an emotional decision-making mode.

Financial Independence Number

The financial independence number is where you are free from the necessity to work. Some people want to retire based on the amount of assets and investments they have accumulated rather than based on age.

This number is best developed with a financial planner if you want to go this route.

Problems and Solutions

Where do business ideas come from? Why are inventions created? Quite often, it is because someone had or observed a problem. So, when bad things happen, they might have positive and rewarding outcomes if someone comes up with a solution. Essentially, business is the solving of problems. If there are no problems, no one is working, and there are few opportunities. One of the best ideas I have had come from taking a job I think was below my skill set. If you invest in private business, or even public companies, there are problems. Business doesn't always go as planned. What you want to see are people who can come up with solutions. Problems create opportunities.

Regulation, Compliance, and Corporate Governance

Regulation serves to protect the financial system and investors. Where the financial system has seen de-regulation, disaster has ensued. Compliance ensures that investments or activities follow certain guidelines and are appropriate for an investor. Corporate governance serves to give management guidance on strategy and managing risk. High performing companies embrace strong corporate governance. Weak governance leads to lawsuits, infractions, fines, and problems with stakeholders. There's a very strong argument for regulation, compliance, and corporate governance, as they provide prudence and ethics in business and banking, to mitigate risk.

It's a good idea to understand the regulatory regime and practices of your area of investment. Much of investment is focused on return. It's important in investment to understand the function of mitigating risk. The costs of risk can be very high and can hurt performance.

Schemes and Bad Investments

A scheme is something presented as an investment but isn't really what it seems. The most famous is the Ponzi scheme, where new investor money is used to pay old investors a high return, so that new investors are attracted, often by other investors. Schemes ultimately collapse. This is where the adage, *too good to be true*, generally prevails. If the returns seem really high, or the investment appears to take you outside of the regulatory regime, or it doesn't add up, chances are it's a scheme. Often, schemes ask you to go outside of the regulatory regime, and you find out later why. The protection offered by regulators does not exist.

Time shares as investments are schemes. Promoters show how the property is different than a hotel. That part is valid. Then they sell it in two-week block increments. Take that 2 week number and multiply by 26 and you will see what they are selling you and compare that amount to a comparable condo.

Bad investments come from bad management with flawed execution—a higher valuation than a professional investor would pay. Take condo hotels, for example. Typically, the cost per door is much higher than a hotel operator would pay. The revenue is exaggerated and the expenses understated. The management agreement (written by management) favours management. The condo owner is paid last—the property has many owners that make the business difficult to manage. Most of the owners are not knowledgeable about the business. The inability to sell an investment can also make a bad investment.

The other bad investment tends to be the *"me too"* company. You see this when a company emerges that is very successful, and there tends to be a bunch of companies that adopt the same business model and rarely achieve similar success or market penetration. The original company has the early market mover advantage but also sets the bar for comparison. Everyone else is judged against what becomes the industry standard. In a few years, the *"me too companies"* are almost all gone.

Private Deals and Lending

Private equity deals can offer opportunities; but when investing, consider the control and exit issues. Usually, investing in a private deal, you are giving up control of your money. Are the promoters, people you can trust, and are they competent to handle your money? What is the time frame for a liquidity event? What is the exit strategy? What liquidity options are there if you need to get out sooner? Most people focus on the opportunity and forget about control and exit. I suggest having someone else look at the deal and structure. If you can't afford an attorney to review agreements, then reconsider. Never use or rely on the promoter's attorney.

In private lending, most of the time, someone is coming to you to borrow because they don't have other options. You may think you know someone, but you really don't know someone until you lend someone money. You are typically dealing with someone young or with less than stellar credit to begin with. Enforcing an unsecured borrowing agreement is difficult. You have little recourse but to sue if that person doesn't pay. You can't affect their credit rating unless you have an account with the business and consumer rating agencies. Chasing a friend or family member around to collect is not enjoyable. In lending, assume, for your own personal situation, that the worst will happen. If someone wants to borrow from you, draft your own agreement and have a recourse option. Never use an agreement drafted by the borrower.

If someone is asking for a loan, ask for a business proposal. That task alone will eliminate most would-be borrowers. If you do decline, you can do so on the merits of the proposal—namely the projections or assumptions—rather than a personal rejection. If you do lend, include a recourse clause or explicit consequences for default. Never put yourself at risk lending money, meaning if you can't afford to make a private loan and lose the money, don't do it.

Cutting Your Losses and Dealing with Bad Decisions

Selling is just as important as buying. One of the hardest things to do in investing is to take a loss. Once you recognize a mistake, then cut your losses and move on. I find that sometimes people put far too much time and energy into making a bad choice work. A mistake that gets 80% of your attention is worse than a loss.

Why do you think people hold on to bad investments, bad people, and bad habits? It appears to me that the worse a decision is, the stronger the desire or need to fix or justify, and the results is that you hold on to a bad choice, often with more vigour than a good one. One of the hardest things to admit to and to let go of is a bad decision. Acknowledge to yourself that the decision is unproductive. Forgive yourself. Forgive the other person. Acknowledge the lesson. Move on.

> *"Should you find yourself in a chronically leaking boat,*
> *energy devoted to changing vessels is likely to be*
> *more productive than energy devoted to patching leaks."*
> – Warren Buffett

Selling Your Business

Selling your business is a way of monetizing what you have created. Selling a business is also a highly emotional event. It is often a key component of building a person's net worth. I have seen people turn down offers for a better offer that never came. How would you feel if you turned down $10,000,000, received no further offers, and the market moved on and your technology became obsolete? I have seen this more than once. There is an art to selling, in that whatever you sell has to go up in value for the buyer, and that means you are giving up some of that future return. If what you are selling isn't going up in value, why would anyone buy? If selling your business is a key component of your wealth strategy, it is a good idea to have professional advisers to assist you.

Other People's Money

Opportunities present themselves constantly. If you are looking for investors to act on opportunities, money is not hard to find. Money is not necessarily what you are looking for. You are looking for people with money, who will act or do the kind of transaction that you are looking to do. *Smart Money* doesn't put all its eggs in one basket. You have to consider your prospective investor's net worth or liquidity. In terms of liquidity, if you are looking for $100K, then you are looking for someone with at least $1M in liquidity.

Be careful in outlining your target investor, because there are many interested investors that like to hear stories but never invest. It is much more frustrating if you do a numbers game and produce no numbers. Investors can also offer more than just money. They can offer advice, or connections, or solutions to problems.

Understand this about people. There's a misconception that everyone wants to make more money. The wealthier people become, the less incentive they have to make more; and they often become preoccupied with preserving capital, which is just another way of saying *not losing money*. Inaction for them is simply better than losing money. If your strategy to create wealth is using other people's money, be clear about your proposition, follow through on what you outlined, and be accountable to your investors. Getting money does not mean your job is done. Getting the money is just a beginning. If you don't manage investors well, by being accountable and producing the results you said you would, you won't grow.

"He that is of the opinion money will do everything may well be suspected of doing everything for money."
– Benjamin Franklin

Raising Money

In raising money, consider that it's a process, not an event. There are essentially four steps: ...

Interest - To get an investor interested in your proposition, you'll need a presentation and a short pitch. You should also qualify the investor at this step for fit and suitability. Are you a match? Often the only criteria a seeker has is money and the relationship between promoter and investor takes a sour turn because there wasn't enough attention spent on qualifying the investor.

Due Diligence - Look for the investor to engage in due diligence and receptivity. Receptivity means engagement, asking questions, talking to a lawyer or accountant. These are signals you have moved to the next step.

Negotiation - The investor is looking at the fine details and may adjust your proposition and make a commitment. A commitment should be part financial.

Close - The final stage is the actual close, which means money in the bank. The transaction is not closed until you have the money.

Since there are multiple steps, there are several places where things can break down. Most seekers get hung up on interested investors. Those are the ones that will just take up your time and not move forward.

In dealing with other people's money, think Competence, Character, and Credit Worthiness. Operate entirely with integrity. You don't want to find the value of integrity by finding out people don't think you have it.

Aim to exceed expectations. Trust is the most important thing for people to move forward with you, and once you break someone's trust, it really doesn't matter what the offering is. People won't invest or do business with someone they don't trust.

Another big mistake people make in raising money is thinking and acting like raising money is the final goal. Once you have raised the money, the real work begins. Now you have to perform and deliver to the expectations you set You have to be accountable and transparent. That means providing updates, statements, and work product. You now have investors as bosses. You have to treat them as such. If you do a good job of managing investors, you will get referrals; but a bad job will have investors liquidating as soon as they get the chance, and a terrible job will have you in lawsuits.

Friends and family are often a source of funds. Do not think you can be casual when it comes to their money. Be extra diligent and accountable. In accountability, show statements, documentation, work product, etc. Friends and family often invest on trust, and if something goes wrong, or they feel left out of the loop, their reaction will be very strong. Family relationships and friendships can be painfully ended over money, so be extra careful.

Brand

What does brand and branding have to do with wealth and investing? Creating a brand creates value for a product or company. Take, for example, Apple: it's a company with a brand for product excellence and elegance, and it is the most valuable company in the world. Branding can do the same for people: Bill Gates, Warren Buffett, and Elon Musk. These are all people with a brand. They don't need an introduction. They don't need a resume. When they want to raise money, people take out their cheque books. If you want to enhance the value of your business, your company or yourself, invest in or create your brand.

What do people have to say about you? Are you reliable? Are you smart? Are you trustworthy? Do you execute as you outline? Do you meet expectations? How do you get yourself branded? Aim to *exceed* expectations, and then create "Wow" experiences for people. Increasing your personal, your product or company brand will increase your wealth. When people say, "Wow," about you, then you are branded.

"Wow."
– Owen Wilson

Creating wealth is essentially leveraging your money and time. This chapter has outlined much of background knowledge. There are so many ways of creating wealth. Key to creating wealth is setting goals. From your goals, set out what you need in knowledge and resources and develop a methodology for your wealth creation.

Goal
What is your most important goal in creating wealth?

How much do you want to accumulate?

Knowledge
Do you have the necessary knowledge? How are you going to develop knowledge, or access knowledge or advice?

Resources
Do you have some money to put to work?

Action
You have to act. You can't just look at deals or listen to pitches.
Do you have a methodology or system? How do you plan to create wealth?

Which investments are you planning to use?
(real estate, stock market, financing or lending, or business investment)

What is the most important take away for you in creating wealth?

Words to look up:

Chapter Nine

Giving

"We make a living by what we get. We make a life by what we give."
– Winston S. Churchill

I think there is a misconception about wealth that it must only be measured in quantity. The traditional definition of wealth is an abundance of valuable possessions or money, the state of being rich, material prosperity, or plentiful supplies of a particular resource. A simpler definition of wealth is "the condition of being happy and prosperous," or "spiritual well-being." In this definition, wealth is achievable by many. The more common understanding involves the notion of "abundance of possessions or of valuable products." In our culture, millionaire or billionaire is the title of wealth.

"If we command our wealth, we shall be rich and free. If our wealth commands us, we are poor indeed."
– Edmund Burke

Humans are unique in the concept of wealth. With wealth, there are well-developed principles and practices on giving and sharing resources. The practice of giving is universally regarded as a virtue or an act that proves humanity and transcendence.

There are several ways to consider giving. I like to look at religion, as I think that it addresses the thoughts and values of people, and stands the test of time. Politics, countries, and empires come and go. Religions last for thousands of years; and, for this reason, I believe that they warrant examining. You don't have to believe in God or ascribe to any religion to examine the principles and teachings. I like history and philosophy, and religion combines the two.

Buddha considered giving from the frame of mind of giving and the recipient with karmic benefits in the present and in the future. According to Buddha, more important than the gift being given is the intention and state of mind when giving. The ideal conditions of giving are to give a pure gift (honestly earned), with pure intentions (no agenda), to a pure recipient (a virtuous and worthy person). The joy of giving would prepare the giver to attain higher aspects of enlightenment. Buddha himself was a prince who abandoned his wealth to purse a spiritual path.

"Before giving, the mind of the giver is happy;
while giving, the mind of the giver is made peaceful;
and having given, the mind of the giver is uplifted."
– Gautama Buddha

For Hindus, giving (*Dana*) is an important part of one's *dharma* (religious duty). *Dharma* has a broad meaning of eternal law, duty, conduct, behaviour, morality, and righteousness. Every person has a *dharma* towards family, society, the world, and all living things. Giving that is motivated by selfish considerations loses its value from the spiritual point of view. For Hindus, there is no point in worshipping *Brahman* (Supreme Being) in all creation while ignoring the needs of others. Charity is more than merely giving; it involves the sharing with others, be it wealth, food, or other resources.

Tikkun Olam is the goal of the Jewish people, to *"repair the world"*. Under this concept, Jews are not just responsible for their own moral and material welfare, but the welfare of greater society. They have a purpose to perfect the world under the sovereignty of God.

Tzedakah is based on a Hebrew word, *Tzedak*, meaning fairness, justice, or righteousness, but it is commonly used to signify charity. *Tzedakah* refers to giving as an obligation to do what is right and just, and it applies to all, not just the wealthy. Originally, those who had more were to leave crops standing in the corners of fields to allow the poor to harvest what they needed. *Tzedakah* is more than giving money to the poor. *Tzedakah* requires the donor to give with the hand and the heart, to share compassion and empathy, along with the money. The recipient should not bear disapproval or criticism.

Under Christianity, a popular verse on giving is Luke 6:38. *"Give, and it shall be given unto you; good measure, pressed down, and shaken together, and running over, shall men give into your bosom. For with the same measure that ye mete withal it shall be measured to you again."* This passage refers to more than just wealth; it refers to all aspects of giving.

Jesus taught giving in several parables or stories. One parable (Matthew 20:1–16) is that of the workers in the vineyard. The vineyard owner hires workers in the morning, and then, throughout the day, hires more. Some work a full day, others a half or a quarter of a day, and others an hour. At the end of the day, the owner first pays the last worker hired, a full wage. The other workers complain amongst themselves. Why does the owner give the person, who does the least work, a full day's wage?

What is Jesus teaching here? Is this socialism? Is this rewarding doing less work? Is this giving to those that don't deserve it? Is this recognizing that all needed the same to provide for their families? If you pay someone a full day for a part day, are you a fair employer? Was this employer giving charity to those in need? The parable doesn't give an answer but an example, with the answer left to be interpreted. Maybe it is a question that is not meant to be answered, but discussed.

Jesus, as a teacher, provided a few other parables about giving. There is the parable of the Good Samaritan who saved a beaten man, while others, who one would expect to help, passed the injured man (Luke 10:30–37). The Samaritan not only helped the man, but paid an innkeeper to care for him. Here, he teaches to treat others and give as you would to yourself.

Another parable is the sower who casts seed to the birds, seed on rocky soil, thorny soil, and rich soil, and ends up with abundance 30, 60 or 100 times despite his waste. (Matthew 13:1-23, Mark 4:1-20, and

Luke 8:4-15). Another curious example. Jesus was not teaching agriculture. Is this an allegory of how given the word how different people understand and receive the message of God? Or is it how people create abundance despite mistakes or waste.

Jesus used parables to illustrate and allow people to come to answers. That is a far more engaging process. To this day, people still discuss the meaning and interpretation of his stories.

With Zoroastrianism, the purpose in life is to "be among those who renew the world ... to make the world progress towards perfection." Its basic maxims include: *Ahura*, The Lord Creator, and *Mazda*, Supremely Wise.

- *Humata, Hukhta, Huvarshta*, which mean: Good Thoughts, Good Words, Good Deeds.
- There is only one path, and that is the path of Truth.
- Do the right thing because it is right and then all beneficial rewards will come to you.

Several *ahadith*, sayings of Muhammad, refer to deep affection and brotherhood: "You will not believe until you love for your brother what you love for yourself." "The believers are like one body in their mutual love and affection: if one limb is injured, the rest responds with sleeplessness and fever." Under Islam, Allah wishes Muslims to feel the suffering of others and have compassion, to share and give charity to ease suffering. Islam emphasizes the spiritual need of those with wealth: to give to remember that they are humble before Allah and that every blessing comes from Him.

Zakat (charity) is the third pillar of Islam and it is a religious obligation for all Muslims who meet the criteria of wealth to make a mandatory charitable contribution of $1/40^{th}$ or 2.5% of their excess wealth. Under the threshold of wealth is *Nisab*, which is for all to make a minimum contribution in money or deed.

In Islamic teachings, there is a positive outcome of giving in charity. When you spend money, the laws of subtraction apply. With charity, there is a subtraction of money, but there is always an unexpected return or an increase. According to Islam, charity is the smartest investment you can make. The concept is that when you give, all do better. No one wants to live in a society where people are living in squalor, desperate or committing crimes to survive. Investing in those less fortunate brings society up and creates an environment where there is social justice and harmony.

Under Islam, the benefit of giving comes from Allah. The reward does not come from the recipient, but from Allah and may manifest in many different ways, based on intentions. Giving to those who have less can be a way to get perspective and have gratitude.

Now, in looking at different religions and how they address giving, I invite you to entertain how these thoughts have entered into your thinking and life. Religion is a major factor in mindset. I invite you to see the similarities and beauty of other religions. I see a common theme of helping those in need and sharing resources, and that this expands benefits and wealth.

How God creates wealth and benefits. Much of our institutions of social welfare have come from the belief that sharing and taking care of others is good for society. I like to look at other religions to see the way that they address the same issues as the one that I was brought up in. I think that understanding different perspectives helps you understand different mindsets and perspectives. The more you understand people, the better you will be at relationships, negotiating, and team work.

What We Have Been Given

First, in wealth, I like to think of what we have been given. We have the benefit of generations of wisdom. We know a great deal about science, health, geology, chemistry, biology, and technology. Every generation builds on the knowledge of the previous. There is a great deal of value in the wisdom that was just given. With every generation, our standard of living in the Western world has been improving.

We have the benefit of social, energy, and transportation infrastructure. We have institutions for health and education. We have justice and the rule of law. We have the benefit of a tax collection system.

We have a democratic process. We have a great deal to be grateful for. All of these things contribute to our lives and the ability to create wealth.

Why is Giving in a Financial Plan?

"Thousands of candles can be lighted from a single candle. Happiness never decreases by being shared."
– Gautama Buddha

"For it is in giving that we receive."
– Saint Francis of Assisi

Why is giving important to creating wealth? What do I mean about giving? Am I referring to charity? Giving to charity is an important part of creating a greater good, and a part of many peoples' giving plans.

My notion of giving is spreading good in the world—creating good that is not exclusively for your benefit. Giving or creating good will create wealth, and in benefiting others, you also serve to benefit yourself.

People are social and complex creatures who need relationships. It would follow that there is a high value in developing and maintaining relationships. A key component and determinant of a relationship is trust. If you trust someone, you are somewhat in a relationship; and when we don't have trust, we have fear and anxiety. With fear and anxiety, this is where things break down. Trust is a powerful economic force that is a key determinant in whether a country, company, or person will get investment or other benefits.

There is an expression that *"You are always selling."* A key attribute of the sales process is the establishment of trust. In this way, I like to think you are always giving. You need to give something of value, to get what you want of value, in almost every relationship.

There is another expression: *"You can't get something for nothing."* Meaning, you have to give something to receive something of value. There are many people that put considerable effort into propositions where they are not willing to invest time, money, or effort; the value on the other side is generally the same. When someone suggests a success-only proposition, it generally tells me that the promoter has so little faith or belief in success that the risk is hardly worth the effort. Mathematically, you have to give something to get something.

The employer gives a wage, and the employee gives time, labour, and intellect. When one job is created, it creates seven other jobs, by the power of one person receiving money, and that money in turn being spent and turned over. In the relationship between employer and employee, both are giving something to each other, which improves the collective good. Part of our strategy in wealth is giving to the collective good. You choose a career; you develop business with an idea and intent of giving something of value and of benefit to others.

Why Giving? The Consequences of Inequality

What is wealth when you have a beautiful home, but when you step outside and there is violence, insecurity, and fear? There is a selfish component to giving, and that is to keep people from taking your stuff or killing you for it.

There is a coefficient that measures inequality. Statistician and sociologist, Corrado Gini, developed an economic construct, the Gini Coefficient, which is a measure of statistical dispersion of the income or wealth distribution of a nation's residents.

The Gini Coefficient measures the inequality among values of a frequency distribution for levels of income. The higher the Gini coefficient, the greater the difference between poor and wealthy; and the lower the coefficient, the more clustered the distribution. A Gini coefficient of zero expresses perfect equality, where all values are the same and where everyone has the same income.

Poverty

There are different types of poverty: abject or real poverty, and relative poverty. Abject poverty is where you do not earn enough income to provide the necessities to sustain life. Relative poverty is where you compare yourself to someone else and feel impoverished or deprived.

You might have a job and housing but still feel poor in relation to those you perceive to have more or a standard you have set for yourself.

What does inequality mean? It means difference in size, degree, and circumstance. According to Dr. Martin Daly, of McMaster University, inequality predicts homicide rates "better than any other variable." According to the World Bank, the connection is so strong that a simple measure of inequality predicts about half of the variance in murder rates between American states and between countries around the world.

What does this mean? It means you are statistically safer from violent crime where almost everyone is poor, where almost everyone is rich, or where almost everyone is middle class. Where there are greater differences in wealth distribution is where you are more likely to run into trouble. Stanford historian, Walter Scheidel, found that high inequality has been reduced through catastrophe: disease, famine, world war, societal collapse, or communist revolution. When inequality becomes high, you see cities, countries, empires, and societies collapse.

When inequality is high, it affects behaviour. Inequality strips people of traditional status symbols—like a good job or the ability to support a family. In these circumstances, matters of respect and disrespect become exaggerated. Small infractions, where someone feels disrespected, end up with disastrous consequences: think of stabbings, because of bumping into someone or road rage. These may seem minor incidents with major consequences.

When you reduce opportunities for respect, status, and personal advancement, people will find less desirable ways to pursue those things. Where there is higher inequality, social reputation becomes more important, and people are more likely to resort to violence or coercion to get their way, as they don't believe that the system will allow them to succeed the moral route.

I bring up Jesus' parable of the vineyard owner, to look at it again. Maybe the reason Jesus suggested that the owner gave all the workers the same amount was because the owner knew that the consequences of inequality would be worse. The Inequality Coefficient was discovered and proved by Gini in 1912, but may have been understood by Jesus, 2000 years ago. A parable doesn't give a definitive answer. For me, this parable raises more questions than it gives answers.

Now, you might ask, should we have no inequality? That is not what I am suggesting. A zero Gini coefficient, where everyone is the same, is simply not achievable. Where societies have tried to enforce equality, it has been disaster, enforced by government tyranny, military or police suppression. Communist governments have torn societies and countries apart, and millions have perished.

A certain amount of competition is beneficial to society—it encourages entrepreneurship, arts, and discussion. Too much competition and inequality, creates social and societal dysfunction and violence; and at extremes, societies collapse, and you see civil and inter-country war, or an arms race to the bottom. I just want you to be aware of the results of inequality and see it when it presents itself. Fairness in the distribution of resources comes at a cost but has its benefits.

The parable of the vineyard owner is one reason I consider religious stories and texts to have some merit. Parables, as a means of teaching, invite you to examine the possibilities and come to an answer. The advice that they give and values they present have stood the test of time. That isn't to say that people don't abuse religion. That is people, not the texts and lessons, at work. Looking at something as defined by its worst members is not a good way to look at anything.

When I discussed mindset, understanding religion is worthwhile. One, there are similarities and differences. Religion goes across all strata of a society and transcends time. Politics are worth understanding. A great deal of our society has been shaped by religion, whether we care to acknowledge it or not. Before governments provided social services, they were provided by churches. Social justice and social welfare— "In God We Trust"—have origins in religion.

I also like to see what religion has in common; a desire to give and provide charity seems to be part of all. The common elements seem to be tithing or mandatory giving, intention and giving for the benefit of others rather than yourself. The notion is that charity benefits the giver and the receiver, even though, mathematically it might not seem the case.

I would like to think that you can do better than giving to benefit ourselves. In benefiting others, it serves a greater good. You are part of and participating in that good. There is a huge value to peace, security, and justice. There is a value to social programs, compassion, and health. Just because you don't need education, justice or health services at a given time, doesn't mean you won't need them to be there for when you do or even if you never need them. If you look at the value of real estate in peaceful and secure countries, it commands a higher price than in less secure countries. More peaceful countries attract more investment and have lower costs of money, so their advantages create greater opportunities.

History tells a repeating story of misery unfolding. History tells us of the exit of Jews from Egypt, the French revolution, the Bolshevik Revolution, the Chinese Cultural Revolution, several Communist revolutions, the American Revolution, the Irish troubles, and the breakdown of European colonialism in Africa. There are far too many examples of the price of misery. The price of misery is much higher than any investment in education, sustainable employment, justice, or health. Still, the tyranny of misery marches on. It's a story that plays out over and over again.

Abject Poverty

What is abject poverty? Abject poverty is starvation or working to death. It's selling children into marriage or prostitution, for lack of better choices. It's human trafficking or slavery. It is the absence of justice, arbitrary incarceration, or execution. It is children uneducated. It is orphaned children raising siblings. It's people dying from treatable diseases. It is refugees and civil war. It's the ugly side of the human condition. It is the inequitable distribution of resources and the problems capitalism doesn't seem to solve.

There is another side of poverty: the more disadvantaged a person is, the harder it is to escape poverty. Moving up the ladder is not a linear task. The higher you start out, the easier it is to get to the next rung. When you look at people, you may think they are where they are because they're lazy and stupid. I believe poverty is not a choice anyone wishes to make. It's a situation that, once in, is very difficult to escape because there are more things working against you.

The other part of poverty is, the more disadvantaged you are, the worse you are likely to be treated. There is something in the human psyche that can turn ugly when someone is vulnerable. It happens in the animal world and it applies to people. The most vulnerable suffer the worst treatment. The vulnerable are subject to more mental abuse or extreme violence or exploitation.

Contempt is a feeling that someone is below consideration. The phrase, *contempt of court*, means disregarding the authority of the court. The court needs respect to function. Sometimes contempt comes about from someone performing below expectation. Sometimes it is a view that a class or race of people is beneath you. The opposite of contempt is respect, to hold in high regard or reverence. Many problems arise from contempt. If there's one emotion that is the kerosene to the human condition, it is contempt. Contempt goes hand in hand with inequity. It goes hand in hand with abuse. It goes hand in hand with war. Much of the fear of failure has to do with the loss of respect. Intuitively we know that there are consequences to contempt and falling out of favour or losing respect.

Misery is a seed for more misery. Desperate people do desperate things. I would like to think that we help others because it is the right thing to do. The economics of helping people in extreme situations is such that it is a less expensive option than terrorism or civil war.

"No one has ever become poor from giving."
– Anne Frank

The Creation of Wealth

What happens when wealth is created at the expense or suffering of others? History has repeated itself so many times. Misery rises up and takes out the tyrant or the cause of misery. The cause of misery might be the ruling or wealthy class, or a dictator, or an exploitive capitalist or colonial system. Why can't we see this?

I believe this stems from a view of wealth and its creation, and a view of winning and losing. For you to win, someone else has to lose. This just doesn't have to be the case. When you sell a stock or a home, the person buying is expecting it to go up in value. You sell and pass something on for someone else to make money.

If you look at the world and the creation of wealth that has taken place over the past century, doesn't it strike you as odd that people are starving, unable to meet the basic standard of living? I believe that there is a view of scarcity; that I have to get mine and keep others from getting mine. I will build as much of mine as I can. I am building only for me and my family.

This type of thinking is why there is corruption and poverty. When life is really hard and competitive, people get selfish and focus on saving themselves and their family. Corruption happens. Violence happens. All of these things make investment and development much harder. The cycle of poverty and underdevelopment goes on and on.

One of the biggest determinants of economic prosperity is trust. And the lack of trust is its greatest deterrent. It follows that a major task of leadership is building trust and relationships. Is this what you are seeing? I think we are seeing a breakdown of trust in government, banking, and police. How is this playing out for our society?

Motivation

I have found that people's motivations to do things are not so much for themselves but for others. Parents work hard to provide for their families and save for their kids' education. One client, a very humble and unassuming man, amassed a net worth of about $20 million through real estate investing. When he spoke of what he did, he always prefaced that what he did was for his wife. He was basically educated in Northern Ontario and worked as a labourer. He was not at all what you would expect in a multimillionaire, but he still achieved a great deal more than most, simply because he wanted to do something for his wife.

Giving

"You can give without loving, but you cannot love without giving."
– Amy Carmichael

When I separated with two young children, I was in difficult financial straits. I used to go to the St. John Mission on Broadview that held a community dinner for women and families. One time, I went, and there was a man who was often around. He was waiting for someone to help him with his hand. The skin around his knuckles had cracked open. I just said, "I have a cream that can help that." I put zinc diaper cream on everything. I thought I would just come back later with the cream. Instead, he just asked me where I lived. I lived close by, and I told him my address. So, I went home. To be honest, I was a little worried, because I had just given a homeless man my address. He did show up, and our exchange was as normal as anyone turning up at my door. I got the cream and put it on his hand. He thanked me and was on his way. Afterwards, whenever he would see me, he would go through his belongings packed on his bike to find something to give me. I thought that it was so profound that here was someone homeless, and he still wanted to give me something.

Giving is a part of a wealth strategy, and a skill, because you are part of something greater than yourself. You care about your ancestors, and you care about our heirs. You are a citizen. You have received and, in return, you give. It is in giving something of value to others that you create wealth.

Social Skill

Giving or sharing is one of the first skills taught to toddlers. It speaks to the importance of social skills, the distribution of resources, and the development of relationships and trust. As a social skill, there are definitely people known for giving and hospitality. Many cultures pride themselves on hospitality. Giving and sharing are clearly important skills for personal success and our social structure.

Giving as a Skill

If giving is a skill and part of the code, how can you give better? There are five key skills in giving:

Giving by Example

"If we could change ourselves, the tendencies in the world would also change. As a man changes his own nature, so does the attitude of the world change towards him. We need not wait to see what others do."
– Mahatma Gandhi

Be an example of behaviour that you want to see. If you want something to be in effect in your life or the world, then lead by example. Talk the talk, walk the walk. Be a good person. Encourage and compliment. Pick up litter. Speak up when someone says something disparaging. Return the change when someone makes a mistake. Be responsible. Be kind. Be appreciative.

Giving by Participation

"Coming together is a beginning; keeping together is progress; working together is success."
– Henry Ford

You might not be able to give money, but you can still give. You can volunteer at school or participate in church. The goal of one becomes the efforts of several and the goal becomes realized with participation. Depending on how large the organization, amplify giving through the actions of many. If you don't feel that you can give money, you can give along the way: in work, in parenting, in community, in school, in church. Large changes are often the culmination of small actions of many people. Together, people are powerful and can effect change, with each person contributing in a small way.

Contribution of Talent

You don't have to be an Olympic athlete or a Michelin chef. You have talents, things that you are good at that others appreciate and benefit from. By giving and contributing our talents we are better and stronger as a society.

Small Acts and the Law of Accumulation

"If you cannot do great things, do small things in a great way."
– Napoleon Hill

Small acts of giving have a cumulative effect. In most religions, you are asked to believe the unbelievable. I am going to ask you to believe that giving helps you create wealth. So how is giving important to the creation of wealth?

There is a theory of the broken window. One broken window attracts more broken windows. More broken windows attract decay and poverty. Decay and poverty attracts crime. So, back to giving and creating wealth, it would follow that small acts of giving could have a cumulative effect.

I'll give you an example: One thing I have noticed about poorer neighbourhoods is a lack of gardens. If you're in a wealthy neighbourhood, you'll notice the curb appeal of nice gardens. If you drive through social housing, there'll be next to no landscaping. Why? It's easier for property management to maintain grass. I have often wondered if we could improve things by just planting gardens. Make things beautiful. I plant things where they weren't for this very reason. Sometimes I pull weeds when I am walking the dog. I'm a secret guerilla gardener.

A garden takes what is good: it takes seeds; it takes sun and water; and it grows. It grows so much that you have to trim it back. It gets weeds, and it takes care, but it shows abundance. Your garden grows, and then you have more than enough. You have vegetables to give to the neighbours. You have flowers for people to enjoy.

"Don't judge each day by the harvest you reap
but by the seeds that you plant."
– Robert Louis Stevenson

"Happiness doesn't result from what we get but from what we give."
– Ben Carson

Forgiveness

Forgiveness is one of the hardest things to have and to give. It is a little easier when someone is sorry. The hardest to forgive is the one without remorse. Much of our sense of justice and fairness is through penalty and retribution. Justice and fairness are concepts that are never concrete. Forgiveness is something you give, not just to relieve the other person; it is something that you give yourself. In forgiveness, you release yourself from the conflict with that person. You forgive to allow yourself to move on.

"Resentment is like drinking poison
and then hoping it will kill your enemies."
– Nelson Mandela

"Darkness cannot drive out darkness; only light can do that.
Hate cannot drive out hate; only love can do that."
– Martin Luther King, Jr.

Responsibility

Noun 1. the state or fact of having a duty to deal with something or of having control over someone. 2. the state or fact of being accountable or to blame for something. 3. the opportunity or ability to act independently and make decisions without authorization.

"The price of greatness is responsibility."
– Winston Churchill

"There are two primary choices in life: to accept conditions as they exist, or accept the responsibility for changing them."
– Denis Waitley

How does responsibility come under *giving*? Responsibility is a gift you give others. You are saying, "I will take care of this." You act in a manner in your personal, business, or professional life that is a benefit to others. You live a life that considers things or matters other than yourself. People can rely on you.

Responsibility is also a gift you give to yourself. Becoming responsible is a step in maturity and a way to respect. You start out incapable of responsibility; then, as a child, you learn small responsibilities, or the consequences of irresponsibility. Look at the happiness of a child given or mastering a responsibility. Education, work, sports, arts—you take on more and more. Eventually, you have and take care of your family because you are mature and capable.

Some people look at responsibilities as burdens. They want the results or benefits of something but not the responsibility. They want a relationship, but they aren't willing to invest time and respect, and getting to know someone. They want a prestigious job but aren't willing to pay their dues. They want rights, but not the responsibilities that go with those rights.

In the pursuit of wealth, what is the role of responsibility? Look at successful people and their thoughts and actions on responsibility, and you will have your answer. Every successful person I know I would describe as responsible. You start by being responsible for results. When you are responsible for results, you get results. By being responsible or more responsible, you are giving to others.

Giving with Intention

"Creation's gold mine is in you. The key is deliberate intention. Whatever your dream may be at this moment, identify it. If you cannot define your desire, it can never become a reality."
– Mary Manin Morrissey

Is *giving* a skill that you can improve on? I believe that skill is *giving with intention*. This is where you have made an observation, a plan, and an idea of the goal you want to achieve. Like all of the skills, you execute with awareness, discipline, and a plan. That plan may be to give to charity—an organization that has structure and programs. Without intention or structure, giving an amount of money, like $25,000, doesn't necessarily solve a problem, but through the Unstoppable Foundation, giving $25,000, with the goal and intention of addressing five areas of development, a community can be transformed. Through intention, an idea given resources goes through execution to results.

Parenting is full of intention. You give love; time, money, and advice, with the intention of helping a young person develop. You help them develop goals. You set aside money for education. You contribute, teach, and encourage skills and responsibility.

Intention is a mental state that represents a commitment to carrying out an action or actions in the future. Intention involves mental activities such as planning and forethought.

Giving to Solve Problems

In giving, it is important to understand that money alone doesn't solve problems. People solve problems. Have you seen a natural disaster where there is a huge influx of money, but the problems of the people and infrastructure don't really improve? This is because, without a comprehensive plan, money gets squandered. Without leadership, the execution may be misdirected. Corruption and poor infrastructure can confound the problems. To solve really big problems, you need planning and cooperation. Large amounts of money do not solve problems.

I believe people are the hands of God. Money is an efficient way to get things done. It puts resources in the hands of people. Those resources need a plan for execution. In many cases, addressing one problem opens up multiple problems. Some of those problems are solved with relationships, understanding, and affection—not a product.

Giving and the Idea of Abundance

Giving also taps into abundance. I believe that there are really two things in all business, money, and energy. You may believe that resources or money is scarce. You only get ahead by someone else's loss. It's a dog-eat-dog world.

You can see this mentality play out in our society. There are people who believe that the success of others is at their expense. Good paying jobs are to the detriment of a corporation. Immigration is to the detriment of nationals. The obsession with the lowest price has been to the detriment of our economy that has led to margins to be compressed to the point where business for suppliers is barely profitable or not sustainable.

Business is just like anything else. You solve a problem; you receive compensation. There is no shortage of problems to solve. There is no end of money and resources. There is a finite amount of oil in the ground, but there is endless energy around us: sun, wind, water, geothermal. You are only limited by your imagination. With abundance, all can participate and receive a fair share for their contribution.

Money Multiplier and Job Creation

While shopping, my daughter Brenna at age 8, remarked to me, "Spending money is good because you get money back". My first thought was, that she could quite possibly become Minister of Finance. She saw me getting change, so in her mind, I was getting money back. She just didn't understand that the change was less money.

What happens when a job is created? What happens when money is spent? There's a multiplier effect. When you get a job, you have spending money, and you pay taxes. When you spend money, the receiver then, in turn, spends part of the money. And so on.

There are many different numbers to suggest one job creates between two and 15 jobs. A common number picked is seven. One job creates or supports seven jobs. So, you can see why, in an economic downturn, the government might spend to stimulate job creation. In an emerging market, you can see the impact of new jobs can dramatically improve circumstances. Job creation is one of the greatest returns on investment, and a social and economic stabilizer. The corollary is that one job lost, it affects seven. This is why concentrated unemployment can be so problematic.

Money and Inequality

Since money is a construct, it's a notion we all agree on. There's no really limit to money. There are billions sitting in bank accounts. Then in turn, there are trillions out in loans. Crypto currencies have been created with block chain encryption, with multi-billion-dollar market values.

What is the root of inequality? Why is there still such an uneven distribution of wealth? There is abject poverty and extreme wealth. That's the big problem to solve. That's achieved by planting the seeds. We need to be moving people to sustainable living with earning income. We can then move them to have savings so they can think of a future. We can then move them to create wealth. We can then move them to give and plant more seeds so that their community thrives. This is putting the ESCG™ code in practice to alleviate poverty.

Giving is an important part of wealth for other reasons. Just as you receive benefit from what came before us, we transfer or give to the next generation. You give to receive compensation. You give to relieve inequality and have peace and security. You give to have trust and good relationships.

Gratitude, Grace, Generosity, and Goals

So, in giving, what should you consider?

Gratitude

> *"Be thankful for what you have; you'll end up having more.*
> *If you concentrate on what you don't have,*
> *you will never, ever have enough."*
> – Oprah Winfrey

> *"As we express our gratitude, we must never forget that the highest*
> *appreciation is not to utter words but to live by them."*
> – John F. Kennedy

Whatever you've achieved, you've also received assistance to help you achieve. You're in relationship with others. You're in relationship with the world. Be grateful for all that you have.

Grace

> *"A new command I give you: Love one another.*
> *As I have loved you, so you must love one another."*
> – Jesus Christ

What is *grace,* and why is it so amazing? I think that the closest thing to describe *grace* is unmerited favour or unearned benefit. Life is the culmination of many decisions, and some work out and some don't work out. You aren't perfect. You make mistakes. You're forgiven. You move forward. You're fortunate or unfortunate, but you're born on this earth, deserving of love. You're deserving of grace. You deserve to share in the gifts of the earth and give of yourself.

Generosity

Generosity is the gift of abundance. Miser is one letter away from misery. Earlier, I discussed the generous trait. It's important to be skilled in generosity, to give to foster productive relationships. You can be generous with compliments, smiles, and friendship. You can have empathy and compassion. You can give money.

"Being generous without keeping score strengthens your spirit,
keeps you focused on the people who make your business what it is,
and helps breed success."
– Brandon Steiner

Giving as a Goal

For you, giving may be a goal and a measure of success. When you're successful, your capacity to give is much greater than when you started. If you've worked through the steps of earning, saving, and creating, you've likely achieved more than enough to give. ESCG™ at work leads to greater giving.

There are ways that you can act that make things worse or make things better. If we're constantly doing things that are good and for the better, then the tide raises all boats.

"The only person that can stop you from achieving your goal is you.
It all begins with your attitude, and if you walk into something
thinking nothing can tear you down, then nothing will."
– Brandon Steiner

When you're imagining what you want and creating wealth are you often thinking of others or what you can do for them. Many of my conversations about money and wealth with clients have been about their desires for loved ones or the causes they are passionate about.

What giving event gave you the greatest satisfaction? What is your greatest giving goal?

Giving

"Kindness in words creates confidence. Kindness in thinking creates profoundness. Kindness in giving creates love."
– Lao Tzu

"A wise person should have money in their head but not in their heart."
– Jonathan Swift

What are you most grateful for?

What is your greatest passion for change in the world?

What are your most important giving goals?

Words to look up:

Chapter Ten

Success and Results

"Once you make a decision,
the universe conspires to make it happen."
– Ralph Waldo Emerson

Sawubona

It's an African Zulu greeting that means, "I see you." It has a long oral history, and it means more that our traditional "hello." It means, *"I see your personality. I see your humanity. I see your dignity and respect."* In the African village context, where everyone knows one another, it's a powerful representation of understanding.

Sawubona. I see you. I see your anxiety. I see your pain. I see your dreams.

I'm flawed. I've made mistakes. I've rebuilt my finances after major setbacks. I wrote this book for you. A book that I read 25 years ago helped me rebuild my life. Now I want to have 100% success in helping people change their lives. You have spent a bit of time with me, so you might have a sense of my personality.

How did I get here?

There was a time when I worked as an investment advisor. I worked with high net worth sophisticated investors with a unique portfolio structure that I developed. Essentially, I shorted long term Canadian bonds to borrow at a fixed rate and invested in high yield securities. My portfolio construction had an above average return, with low volatility and a built in inflation hedge.

Unfortunately, the financial crisis of 2009 was difficult for me. The financial crisis in the US affected investors globally. Investors were in full-fledged shutdown. Business stalled and so my earnings dwindled. Then came a personal crisis represented by my marriage breakdown. Suddenly, I was a single mother of two children in childcare, while in a straight commission role in the worst market of the century. Stress related health issues made matters even worse. I experienced burnout without the benefit of knowing what I was experiencing. I drew on my savings to cover my living expenses and then basically I had to start over in middle age, single with two children.

I rebuilt myself and my finances. First, by drastically cutting my burn rate. Then, by eliminating debt. And in a much disciplined fashion, I saved 10% of money that came to me. First, in jars. Then, eventually, I put money in the bank.

With this book, I hope to help you set goals and get you started on a financial plan. Through my experiences, I've come to recognize some of the things that stop people from managing their finances.

There are a myriad of messages and more information than a person could possibly digest on the topic of personal finance. That's why I came up with the very simple ESCG™ Code—and a one-page summary of these cornerstones—so you could have absolute clarity.

This is a book on setting goals, and it includes some suggestions on how to manage to get yourself in a position to start a new financial plan—one free of debt, with savings, and on a path to building assets and achieving some of your greater personal goals.

There are several things that determine someone's success in finance. decision-making and personality play a role. Financial literacy is not well taught. That's not an excuse. It's a reason to learn these skills on your own.

The skills of the ESCG™ Code are not big secrets. Earning, Saving, Creating, and Giving. They are just buried in jargon, products, and mixed messages. Now they are laid out for you, as four skills to master, and four cornerstones of your financial picture. You can take a piece of paper, fold it into four squares, and have a clear picture of your finances. If you have a mate or partner, you should each do one and share it, and have a conversation about it. It is much easier for you to discuss a one-page synopsis and see your similarities and differences.

I was asked to provide a workshop, and I put some thought into what I thought were the cornerstones of finance. I felt that if personal finance were presented in a way that was both simple and clear, then it would help people move forward. That is how I arrived with the ESCG™ Code. What it did was help me clarify and focus. So, now it is very easy for me to switch gears as to what I need to work on. I know what my strong skills are. I am very good at saving money. I understand investments. When I focus on something, the solution comes.

The Framework

The first step is to have a framework to understand your financial picture, to help you make a plan and better financial choices. From there, you can make decisions about purchases, or registered plans, or investments, etc. Your financial picture and finance isn't as complicated as you might think. The ESCG™ exercise will prove that to you.

"There is no such thing as failure. There are only results."
– Tony Robbins

*"The future belongs to those who believe
in the beauty of their dreams."*
– Eleanor Roosevelt

Getting Results

Now you have a piece of paper with your goals and financial picture laid out in a simple format. What seemed complicated now seems so simple and straight forward. What are you going to do with this?

139

What I've observed about successful people is that they have advisors or coaches. The next part of your plan is to get yourself working with people who will help you put your plan in action.

Why do people not plan? It's not that people don't plan. The truth is that most people are intimidated by something that does not seem concrete. You need to understand that 20, 30 or 40 years down the road something very real is going to happen. Your income is going to be reduced by retirement, and there must be funds to replace that income if you want to maintain your lifestyle. "What lifestyle?" you might ask. "I'm just living from paycheck to paycheck." Then there's all the jargon of the financial industry. The investment industry provides contrary investment strategies all the time: invest this way, invest that way. Outperform, underperform. Confusion leads to inertia, not action.

I believe that you can start with developing your own picture. The ESCG code puts everything on one page. It is simple, but there is value in simplicity. At a glance, the areas of your life and finances are clear, your goals spelled out. Now it is up to you to come up with the plan to execute.

Earnings: What can you do here? Save and/or make more money.
Savings: Eliminate credit card debt. Save 10%. Save 3 months' expenses.
Creating: How much, and how do I do it? What is your Financial Independence Number?
Giving: What's your motivation and intention?

What is a Financial Plan?

Financial plans are tools financial planners use to provide scenarios of what your financial picture will look like. I want to be clear: the ESCG™ Code is not a financial plan. It is the methodology or design guidance and goals that you can give to an architect to develop a financial blue print.

Financial planners use software to do financial plans. Accounting firms can do financial plans as well. These reports can be quite detailed and take into consideration inflation, compounding, and growth of investments, and can provide scenarios for major life events. There are also online resources that you can use for developing budgets and plans.

"An investment in knowledge pays the best interest."
– Benjamin Franklin

"Good judgment comes from experience,
and a lot of that comes from bad judgment."
– Will Rogers

Responsibility

"One's philosophy is not best expressed in words;
it is expressed in the choices one makes...
and the choices we make are ultimately our responsibility."
– Eleanor Roosevelt

"Concern yourself more with accepting responsibility than with
assigning blame. Let the possibilities inspire you more than the
obstacles discourage you."
– Ralph Marston

You may feel like bad things keep happening to you. You are affected by many things that you may feel that you can't control. You can't control the economy. You can't affect the government. You can't control the weather. You can't affect traffic. Everything you do involves a choice. You can be affected, and that means you can be like a weathervane, spinning with every change of the wind. There are two things you can be: a cause or an effect.

What's responsibility? Responsibility is the ability and willingness to act as if you're the cause. You can decide to be responsible for your choices; and even if you're the affected, take the measures you need or want, to see a positive outcome, even if you weren't the cause. If you wait for the real causes to take positive and meaningful actions, you might be waiting for a long time. Be the cause. There are *reasons* for the things you do, and *excuses* for things you don't.

The number one thing that you can do to improve your circumstances and your future is to accept responsibility for your results and outcomes. There are many excuses and many people will choose to be a victim of circumstance. Responsibility has its challenges but it also has its rewards. When you find yourself giving an excuse, find your reason and cause and take responsibility.

> *"Accept responsibility for your life. Know that it is you who will get you where you want to go, no one else."*
> – Les Brown

Free Advice

The first advice people often get is free. Free advice can be some of the most expensive advice you can get. It may sound as if that person is a successful investor, but if that person is a relative or friend, do your own homework. There are lots of armchair would be hedge fund managers. Everyone and anyone seem to think that they can give financial advice. I've seen people get very bad advice—investment, legal, and accounting—all from well-intentioned free sources that turned out to be expensive advice.

Coaches or Mentors

Many successful people use coaches and mentors, in one or more areas of their lives. Take a lesson from them in this respect. A coach is someone who can help you flush out your ideas and provide feedback. Feedback is important, as even the most intelligent person doesn't see all aspects of a problem.

Your coach or mentor isn't there to pat you on the head or tell you what a great guy or gal you are. Your coach is there to make you accountable, or motivate you, or simply point out things you could be doing better. Someone that you're accountable to is a good thing. It keeps you on track and getting things done. Sometimes your mistakes or faults are pointed out. Own your mistakes. Own your faults. Your coach isn't a miracle worker. You have to do the work, training, or exercise to succeed.

Financial Advice

First off, understand the differences between financial advisors. Investment Advisors are professionals who give advice on a wide range of aspects of finance and securities. They study financials, investments and portfolio management so that they can sell and advise on securities. That doesn't stop you from studying investments. That's how I went into the investment industry. I went from learning about investments and mutual funds on my own. I've met many investors that are very adept at selecting investments. They find an area they're interested in, like mining or real estate, immerse themselves, and are just as knowledgeable as professionals.

I found that many people assumed there was a great deal of overlap or similarity between accountants and financial advisors. They are really quite different. An accountant is more involved in the finance of operations and personal and corporate taxation. The investment advisor is concerned with the finance of valuation and risk. An investment advisor may also be a certified financial planner, which enables him or her to address issues around taxation. A good way of thinking about financial advice is to have an accountant to help you with filing and saving on taxes, and an investment advisor to provide advice on building and preserving wealth and managing risk.

Investment Advice

One of the things I've found about successful and wealthy people is that they have advisors. Take a lesson from them. They may be very knowledgeable about investments, and they may use internet resources, but many wealthy people still use financial advisors. They don't focus on the cost of the doing transactions. The cost of making a mistake makes it worthwhile for them to get professional advice.

Now, why have an investment advisor if you're good at investing? Surely you can find an investment advisor who knows at least as much as you and likely more. There's value in having someone to act as a sounding board and give a different perspective. An advisor may bring opportunities to your attention. You can read books on investing, but often the advice given is general. For example, contribute to your retirement plan or pay down your mortgage. Buy term or whole life insurance. You can read advice on both sides. The point is that an advisor can help you determine solutions for your particular situation. There are more factors in an individual situation than given in general advice.

When investing in the stock market, there are many messages, and often they're contradictory. Even within the same firm, there are contradictory views. Someone is right and someone is wrong. In the next month, that may be reversed. The point I'm making is that there's no definitive right answer, except in hindsight, but the whole message of the investment industry is that there's a definitive right answer. Every fund, every advisor, every newsletter writer, every analyst will tell you they have the answer.

So, what do you do? Set your goals, make choices, and live with them. An advisor can help you sort through all the mixed messages and confusion and help you make choices with confidence. If you want to be successful in investing, you need to stay the course. At times, your investments may underperform, but that can reverse. Excessive switching to chase returns hurts returns. Investing is a patient pursuit.

Compensation

The issue of compensation in managing money is a consideration. The financial industry, in some circumstances, buried its fees in deferred sales charges. The fund companies paid the commission. This has led consumers to believe that someone else should pay for managing their money. It is your money. You should pay for the management of your money so that you have an accurate account of your costs.

Do you buy the cheapest food, clothes, car, or furniture? Do you save money fixing your own car or doing your own home repairs? Investing has costs, and you do need to make a decision on your costs and what you value. There are less expensive ways to invest, and they require effort on your part.

Some people like investing and doing research. I was one of those people, so much so that I did the courses for my securities license. There are people that hate investment research. For them, reading about the stock market is boring. You have to decide what you like and what is fair value to pay for.

The other factor is decision-making. Even well informed people sometimes have difficulty making decisions quickly. In the securities industry, the market changes, and decisions to buy stocks are made on the spot with a short explanation. You may find that this is the biggest challenge. Stock prices vary, and it is extremely rare to buy at the bottom and sell at the top. Your decision-making capabilities will have a great determination on what investment products are suitable for you. If you aren't comfortable making spot decisions, then mutual funds and ETFs are better for you.

Using an advisor is a more expensive option. An advisor provides a service and value, and is accountable to you. An advisor also provides a relationship and an understanding of your situation. An advisor can provide a plan and a means of keeping you on track to achieve your goals.

Accounting Advice

An accountant should help you with savings on your taxes. Some accountants offer investment insight. You might ask an accountant what he or she thinks of projections. You might ask an accountant what they think about an investment opportunity. It's a good idea to establish a dialogue between your accountant and your investment advisor.

Understand, when professional people give advice, they are accountable. So, typically accountants don't give investment advice or insight unless specifically engaged to. When you ask an accountant if you should invest in something it gives the perception by the professional is that you don't understand. In this circumstance, the accountant might be held liable and the answer is almost always no. When I see someone referring to their accountant, I take it as that that person is really looking for someone to say no. You should understand and be responsible for your investment choices and ask your accountant for accounting advice, not investment advice.

Insurance Advice

One of the important aspects of your financial plan is protecting what you have or transferring assets to heirs. It's important to have an insurance analysis done. You can evaluate term or whole life plans. Look at an insurance projection to make your determination.

Real Estate Advice

There is a broad spectrum of realtors. Almost all realtors can sell homes. But commercial and income property realtors specialize in selling investment properties. If you're buying real estate for investment, use realtors who are more knowledgeable about income property investing. It's simply better to use a specialist.

A good investment realtor should be able to discuss net operating income (NOI) and capitalization (cap) rates. A good investment realtor should be knowledgeable about areas from a rental perspective—what appeals to a renter: transit, shopping, and proximity to schools and other infrastructure (hospitals, employment districts, military bases, etc.). A rental property might be in a neighbourhood that you wouldn't choose to live in. Your realtor should understand the type of tenants that the property will likely attract, and the rent market, as well as renovations. A realtor for income properties should be able to make suggestions that make the property appealing, cost effectively. Ask a realtor who deals with investors what tools he or she uses to evaluate properties.

Income property values can be improved by reducing expenses and increasing rents. A good property investment realtor should be able to help you evaluate the current financials. Often, a listing broker will provide pro forma financials, which give you an idea of the property potential—if certain improvements are made. If a property has pro forma financials, the realtor should be knowledgeable enough to evaluate and explain.

Using a realtor who focusses on family homes rather than income properties can be a frustrating experience. This was an early mistake that I made: spending too much time and looking at too many houses with the wrong realtor. I suggest you find someone with investment property expertise. You will get better ideas and service from a specialist than from a generalist.

Mortgage brokers can also be important in helping you finance your investments. A broker can provide solutions from a variety of companies rather than you having to go to multiple banks.

Legal Advice

One area of wealth management that's overlooked is one's estate. No one plans to die, but it happens. As someone who has seen how difficult it is to lose someone, it's far more difficult to lose someone and then have to deal with affairs that aren't in order. A family member had a friend die while working in Oman. He left a wife and young child. Sharia law dictates how an estate is handled. His estate had to be handled by a male relative, so a male family member had to come from Britain to deal with the estate. It made things complicated for his widow.

Basically, if you don't leave a will, the government takes over and distributes your estate. All that you worked to build and transfer is in the hands of government to distribute.

You can handwrite a will, and it's valid in Canada. It is called a holograph will. It is not great, but it is better than nothing. If you have nothing, then handwrite something; sign it and put it in an envelope. Then, go to a lawyer or online and draft something better. There are lawyers who will develop a will very inexpensively. It's a good idea to get some professional advice here, as your legacy and how it's handled can have repercussions for the family. If not enough care and thought is put into your will, it can cause dissension amongst family members. You may update your will with codicils made with your lawyer when you have changes in family circumstances.

Your choice of executor is a key consideration. There is work involved and it helps if the person selected has some financial acumen and the time. You can also hire a professional to act as an executor. The benefit of a professional is that person or entity has the experience, assumes responsibility for settling the estate which reduces the potential for liabilities and is impartial.

When you're undertaking a real estate transaction or private investment, get independent advice. This is a mistake that I've made. The mistake I made was dealing with lawyers who made mistakes. Lawyers are the last people you want to have a legal dispute with. Always, always, always get independent legal advice.

In lawyers, there is a broad spectrum in terms of knowledge, experience, and expertise. Some are transactional, meaning they are really good with contracts and agreements. Corporate, securities, litigation, criminal, or family law are all separate disciplines. A good lawyer understands law. A really great lawyer understands business and people.

Transactional versus Relationship Advisor

Most advisors are compensated by commission. There's an inherent bias in the relationship from the outset. That's just the way the system has been set up. There are salaried advisors. How can you tell if you have a good advisor?

A transactional advisor is one that is focused on getting you to buy. If you want to buy, and you're ready, then a transactional advisor can be helpful. The characteristics of a transactional advisor will be that they emphasize a purchase from the outset, and they have less patience and limited follow up.

Have you ever gone to buy paint or a printer, and agonized over the choices? This is referred to as *Cognitive Dissonance*: holding two conflicting views. You want to buy something, but you don't want to make a wrong choice. Most people experience cognitive dissonance in making minor and major decisions. That's simply anxiety about change and making a choice. A transactional advisor may help you make an informed choice, move forward, and leave satisfied with your choice.

Is there a risk that a transactional advisor is going to advocate a poor product? Look where you're buying. Is it a dodgy dealership or time share seminar, or a broker with a hot stock tip?

A relationship advisor is one that is looking to establish a long term business relationship with you. The initial encounter will be one of getting to know you. A relationship advisor builds a practice, provides information or advice, and is willing to wait for your business. Typically, this type of advisor has been in business for a longer period of time.

With a relationship advisor, it has to be a good relationship. This is where the personalities of both the advisor and client intersect and affect the outcome. It's possible to have a poor and non-productive relationship advisor. It's a poor relationship advisor who allows the client to stay in the research zone and not move forward. It's a poor advisor who thinks that being a doormat is helpful. Having the right advisor should be a great and productive experience.

Be a Good Client

You know who gets great deals from advisers? Good clients. People that respect and appreciate their advisors. If you do nothing but look at deals or ideas, and never act, then eventually you won't get called. Have realistic expectations. Participate in the process, and act on opportunities. If someone is making you money, reward or appreciate them, and they'll make you more money. You want to be the first call when your adviser has a great deal.

Spirituality

*"Science is not only compatible with spirituality;
it is a profound source of spirituality."*
– Carl Sagan

*"Great men are they who see that spiritual is
stronger than any material force—that thoughts rule the world."*
– Ralph Waldo Emerson

Spirituality is the part of us that asks questions. It's the part that allows us to conceive new possibilities. Spirituality is about the connection of humans to something broader or larger. It may push the boundaries of what we know of the physical or scientific world. It's the seat of our goals and aspirations. The inventions of man come into existence because of thought. A tree exists because of a seed. Apple Inc. exists because of the ideas of Steven Jobs. Tesla Inc. exists because of the thoughts of Elon Musk. Thoughts become reality. This book exists because someone gave me a task that made me think about how to solve a problem. The human spirit is the connection of the impossible to the possible.

"Nothing is impossible; the word itself says 'I'm possible!'"
– Audrey Hepburn

"Change your thoughts and you change your world."
– Norman Vincent Peale

Sometimes you need more than motivational quotes and posters. If you want change, that sometimes takes a certain amount of soul searching. I've found that people who are in a great deal of pain— financial or personal—have a tendency to find a medicating solution. They go to their doctor and get a prescription for anxiety or depression. Or they just self-medicate with drugs and alcohol. This allows them to keep doing what brought them to their anxiety or depression. I understand that there can be true depression and mental illness. You also have to realize you can't solve life problems with medication. There is no get out of debt pill.

Part of making change is working through your own motivation—creating the proper attitude, setting goals, and being positive. But breaking old habits is harder than it seems. Sometimes you have to avoid people who are negative influences. I've also found successful people work hard on their thoughts. They may have life coaches. They read books. They may have regimes for positive affirmations, meditation, or prayer. The spiritual aspect of their lives is very important.

When things came crumbling down for me, I did focus on such things. Part of failing was not keeping my head in the game. I let everything negative going on in the markets and my personal life overwhelm me. I believe negative thoughts impacted my health. In my efforts to turn the tide, I focused on positive thinking and weeding out negative thoughts. But I was alone. I was ashamed. I'd failed, and I was broken. I just started to go to church. I hadn't been for years, but when your spirit is broken, it seems like the place to go to be fixed. It was. I was welcomed and supported. My dignity was preserved.

I do suggest that people go to church. Why? Church is a destination of people coming together for a variety of reasons but all participating in a service, music, sharing of stories, prayer, and intention. Part of undergoing change is keeping a positive attitude. When you want to make changes for the better, part of doing that is admitting to failure or less than success, living with your choices, and making new plans. Church is noted for having a positive effect on health.

Often left to your own devices you will entertain negative thoughts or distractions. Church puts you in a place where you spend one hour with other people thinking, singing and praying about how to make the world a better place.

I think we are seeing an epidemic of loneliness. People have replaced social connections with online connections. Some of those online connections are not positive. They can reinforce bad ideas. Tweets and comments don't replace real conversation. Church can give you a connection to people that are kind and welcoming and you can participate and interact as much as you want or need.

> *"A community is the mental and spiritual condition of knowing that the place is shared and that the people who share the place define and limit the possibilities of each other's lives. It is the knowledge that people have of each other, their concern for each other, their trust in each other, the freedom with which they come and go among themselves."*
> – Wendell Berry

Spiritual Advice

So, why is spiritual advice here? The *Smart Money Guide* should be about money, finance, and wealth. Well, the acquisition and management of wealth also has to do with life and living. It has to do with relationships with other people and the world.

> *"Amazing grace! How sweet the sound That saved a wretch like me! I once was lost, but now am found; Was blind, but now I see."*
> – John Newton, 1779

One of the greatest investors, Warren Buffett, had this to say: *"Unconditional love is the most powerful force in the universe. I got unconditional love from my parents ... and I've been blessed in that I love what I'm doing so much that I have no desire to get away. I'm playing in my playground, and I don't let the world decide my schedule."* This man, who is known as the greatest investor of all time, didn't just speak of finance or the stock market. He spoke of the power of love. Essentially, the love he speaks of is of grace, acceptance, and forgiveness.

"When spirituality is the basis of your life, it gives you the strength, wisdom, and courage to surmount the many storms of life that could destroy a weaker person who doesn't have this foundation."
– Radhanath Swami

So, why do I suggest spiritual advice? In life, success lies in discipline—in doing successful things, over and over again—in health, in fitness, in finance, and in life. And having some spiritual guidance can help you crowd out some of the influences that took you off the path that you wanted to be on.

It seems that we may have filled a void in our life with other things—drugs or alcohol, material possessions, power, or work. If I were to ask you the question, *what drives behaviour more, reality or what you think reality is*, what would your answer be? I am going to go with the answer, *what you think reality is.*

The thoughts that are going on in your head are the real drivers; so, by that observation, it's important that you are careful what thoughts you entertain and what you allow to influence your thinking. Negative thoughts and fear are detrimental. Positive thoughts and affirmations are important. When you are positive, it leads to action. When you are negative, it leads to inaction—or worse, negative actions.

Where should you get help to work on your body? You go to the gym. Where should you get help for your health? You go to the doctor. It seems to me, if you want to work on your soul, then you might go to a place that specializes in souls. I've been to numerous churches. I have been to a Russian Orthodox Church, an Asian Christian church, a Diwali ceremony, a Mosque, and the church I was raised with—the United Church.

I found myself in a situation where everything had broken down for me. Part of how I got there was by letting negative thinking overtake me—in my marriage and in my career. Part of getting past that and rebuilding was by putting positive thought into my thinking. I had to turn my thoughts around to get to setting goals and finding a plan to rebuild.

I was alone and with two children. In church, I found grace. I found support without judgement. My dignity was kept intact. People don't realize that some of the reasons people don't get the help they need is because of pride and dignity.

Religions developed because people observed wealth and poverty, power and chaos, and sought to bring some order to their lives and community. People put some thought into how to make things better. They developed stories to explain major life themes. They developed traditions to reinforce their values. Religion tries to provide people with answers about life and how to live it. When you want to execute on a plan, there is a methodology and philosophy already put together for you.

Some may rail against organized religion. It's easy to point out the deficiencies or what has been done wrong. What about all the things done right? The architecture, the art, the music, the organization of people, the development of community, the organization of charities, not to mention the relationships, bringing people together to sing, pray, and worship, to put positive messages into one another's lives, and to articulate their thoughts and plans for a better world. To celebrate achievement or milestones or support in times of tragedy. There is structure, committees, volunteers, and funding mechanisms. When Canadians decided to sponsor Syrian refugees, many church-related organizations provided the sponsorship.

Remember this about organizations of any kind: they are made up of people. People have faults and make mistakes. Corporations, entities or organized religions are made up of people. Essentially, they are a culmination of the attributes and faults. There will be some good and some bad. You can choose what you see more of. I can say that I go to church, not because I am a good person but because I want be a better person.

As I have participated in a wide variety of ceremonies and services, I have met people who are thoughtful, courageous, helpful and intelligent, active and positive, in their pursuit of a greater good. The pursuit of wealth isn't just the pursuit of money; it's a pursuit of a richer life. Your life can be richer with an attention to what's really important to you. I think religion or spirituality can only serve to enrich your life. It may move your focus from the matter to the meaning of life.

Faith

What is faith? I think faith is the belief in the unbelievable. Faith is something that you believe and can't prove. Why do I bring this up? Sometimes, when things were bad, I would get consumed with negativity. I would focus on the negative and the loss, and it would make me very upset and anxious. I would have uncontrollable negative thoughts. Then I would say to myself, "You got it once; have faith that you will get it again, and what will come will be even better."

I'm an analytic person, and I tend to think in probabilities. Many times, I've observed and experienced the improbable. When the improbable happens, then I pay attention. These are the little miracles that give me faith.

One such incident was when my mother died. She died suddenly, and I was not in a good financial position. I didn't have money to buy her a funeral flower arrangement, so I bought a pot of tulips at a market. The tulips I chose were a light pink because I thought that she would like those best. The problem was that the pot was the only one in that colour, and they were green buds. I didn't expect that they would bloom for a week. I thought my brother would be able to plant them to remember her.

I woke up the next day, the day of the funeral. The tulips hadn't just turned colour; they had fully bloomed. Tulips go from green buds, to closed colour, and then open blooms. This takes a couple of days to turn colour, and then a couple of days to open. These tulips skipped the middle step and were in full bloom, from green buds, overnight. I was shocked and pleasantly surprised. Since then, I have bought many pots of tulips, but I have never replicated the speed at which these tulips bloomed

Now, is it possible that these tulips bloomed in one day by natural causes? Based on my experiments with pots of tulips (of which I have bought many), the blooming of these tulips overnight was very improbable. So, those tulips gave me enormous comfort that my small gift was accepted and made beautiful for my mother. It was a small miracle for me.

I have many examples of improbable, and I've come to accept improbable miracles. I took the tulips blooming as reassuring and a sign. Maybe there's a scientific reason, but I like my version better.

At one point, people thought the earth was flat, but Columbus had faith that it wasn't. Galileo had faith that the earth revolved around the sun, and he risked his life and reputation. Think of the first men who went to the moon, who put their faith in projections and the talents of so many people. So, believing in the unbelievable has led to some remarkable steps forward. One day, someone just has an idea that sets the world on its ear, and there are likely more to come.

> *"He, who loses money, loses much; He who loses a friend,*
> *loses much more; He, who loses faith, loses all."*
> – Eleanor Roosevelt

In observing successful people, I have found they paid attention to their thoughts. They have coaches, and some of those are personal coaches, for motivation and spirituality. There are motivational personalities, with books and programs. I can refer some resources, if you would like. Just contact me at **goals@thesmartmoneyguide.com**, and I will send you some good references.

> *"Happiness is not in the mere possession of money;*
> *it lies in the joy of achievement, in the thrill of creative effort."*
> – Franklin D. Roosevelt

You're the one who needs to pay attention to your thoughts, your heart and soul, because money doesn't fill all of your needs. What goes into your head, directs your action. You can pursue distractions. You can focus on actions of achievement. You can pursue wealth. Success for many people in wealth lies in what they can give others. Wealth in itself is a goal, but it goes hand in hand with achievement, meaning and purpose.

Now, I've given you the tools to become *Smart Money*. I have addressed money, goals, decision-making, and personality. I've outlined the ESCG™ Code, which has now made your financial situation clear on a piece of paper: Earning, Saving, Creating, and Giving. I've discussed getting results with the right advisors and coaches. I've made you aware of the importance of your heart, mind, and spirit. I've given you the tools to move forward with a financial plan, with advisors who can coach or mentor you. Now you can put the numbers on your paper.

Additional to the code, I've also outlined other things you need to address. You need *discipline*. One of the biggest factors in success is just doing what works more often, and eliminating what doesn't work. You need *motivation*. You need to have a positive view and expectation of success.

> *"Optimism is the faith that leads to achievement.*
> *Nothing can be done without hope and confidence."*
> – Helen Keller

There are new beginnings to be had at any age or stage of life. The seed of creation is in your mind. I want to sincerely thank you for taking the time you have spent with me. I know, with the ESCG™ Code, you can set your goals and start on your path. Have a foundation. Build from the ground up. Sometimes you want the result, but to get to that result, you need to build, brick by brick. Those bricks need to be on a solid base.

I've discussed *Smart Money*—being aware and knowledgeable about the four skills. Much of your thought about money may have been about what it can buy. *Smart Money* also thinks about what money can do. *Smart Money* is also about who you are.

Who Do You Want to Be?

Smart Money is not just about money and possessions. Part of being successful in money is about who you are—being the person you want to be. Money is a measure. You can manage money better, and you never stop improving. You never stop working on yourself. The coaches and mentors I know, have coaches and mentors.

*"Money is neither my god nor my devil. It is a form of energy
that tends to make us more of who we already are,
whether it's greedy or loving."*
– Dan Millman

*"When your life is possession-centered, the important thing is
what you have; when it is principle centered,
the important thing is who and what you are."*
– Dr. Nido Qubein

*"Of the billionaires I have known, money just brings out the basic
traits in them. If they were jerks before they had money, they are
simply jerks with a billion dollars."*
– Warren Buffett

Failure

You have likely been trained and ingrained that failure is bad and to be avoided. Another way of looking at failure is the demarcation point for competence. You can retreat from failure, or you can look at it as a line to cross. How are you going to do that? Are you going to reassess and try again? Are you going to get a coach to help you with your performance? Are you going to try a different way? Successful people make success or talent seem effortless; but in reality, they have just failed more and pushed their demarcation point further and further.

Regret

There are reasons for the things you do, and excuses for the things you don't. Regret is a hard feeling to deal with, and causes more pain than failure. With failure, at least you know. Regret leaves you wondering what would have happened if you had the courage to try.

Focus

I'm sure you've heard of multi-tasking. This is the opposite of what you should do. You can do a hundred things badly or one thing really well. Which is better? The first will get things done poorly and hurt your reputation. The latter will get you noticed for being excellent at one thing. Focus on one thing at a time. Master the skill or task. Achieve. Then move on.

Now, with respect to the ESCG™ Code, you may need to focus on one area at a time. Awareness of the four areas is helpful to tackle your financial picture. With time and practice, you'll be able to clearly focus on what you need to.

Discipline

Set a regime and stick to it. Do things that lead to success more and more. Do things that lead to failure less and less. Get up in the morning. Have a routine. Be punctual. Make the calls. Small successes lead to bigger successes.

Integrity

Integrity is the quality of being honest and having strong moral principles—moral uprightness. If integrity were easy, everyone would have it. Do the right thing, even if it costs you money. Your reputation is your brand. Your brand is the culmination of your value. It doesn't matter how smart, beautiful, or talented you are, if people don't think you have integrity. Trust is the most important thing in relationships; if you lose or break someone's trust, it is very hard to regain. You do not want to learn the value of integrity by having people believe that you don't have it.

"Real integrity is doing the right thing,
knowing that nobody's going to know whether you did it or not."
– Oprah Winfrey

> *"The high road is always respected.*
> *Honesty and integrity are always rewarded."*
> – Scott Hamilton

Why is integrity so important? Trust is a foundation for all endeavours. Lying is destructive and weakens your efforts. What business is made better by lying? What relationship is made better by lying? What investment is made better by lying? The answer is *none*. The worst lies are the ones you tell yourself, because those are bad seeds. You tell lies, and you may think you'll get away with something. You might even start believing them. With lying, you may cut corners, but you invariably end up telling more lies to cover the first lie, and then you have a house of cards, waiting to fall. What is manifested from the lie grows, but on a false foundation. When it collapses, it is always much worse.

If you make a mistake, tell the truth; take your lumps sooner than later. Someone might be angry or disappointed, but this will be small in comparison to a long, protracted lie. Avoiding problems only allows the problem and the consequences to get bigger.

> *"With integrity, you have nothing to fear,*
> *since you have nothing to hide. With integrity,*
> *you will do the right thing, so you will have no guilt."*
> – Zig Ziglar

Courage

Courage is a word we use all the time, but it bears thinking about. Everyone has fear and doubt. Courage is the quality of mind or spirit that enables a person to face difficulty, danger, or pain. The definition describes it as *without fear*, but I believe courage is about overcoming fear, not eliminating it. In the presence of fear, you are still able to act.

"Before you can become a millionaire, you must learn to think like one. You must learn how to motivate yourself to counter fear with courage. Making critical decisions about your career, business, investments, and other resources conjures up fear, fear that is part of the process of becoming a financial success."
– Thomas J. Stanley, Author of *Millionaire Next Door,*
and *The Millionaire Mind*

Courage is what moves you to action in the face of risk. Courage also unlocks other things within us. Virtues and personal values are based on courage.

"Courage is not simply one of the virtues but the form of every virtue at the testing point."
– C. S. Lewis

"One isn't necessarily born with courage, but one is born with potential. Without courage, we cannot practice any other virtue with consistency. We can't be kind, true, merciful, generous, or honest."
– Maya Angelou

Why does *Smart Money* need courage? It is just like faith. Faith allows you to believe. Courage enables you to act. There is no progress without belief and action. There are material things we value and other things we value—peace, justice, and security. These are luxuries that many people don't have, and they exist because people had the courage to defend them. We often take these things for granted. *Smart Money* isn't just about what you know. It's also about who you are. Part of wealth is the freedom to say no to what you don't want, and live the values you do want.

Attitude

Attitude is a settled way of thinking or feeling about someone or something, typically one that's reflected in a person's behavior.

"Achievers have an enabling attitude, realism, and a conviction that they themselves were the laboratory of innovation. Their ability to change themselves is central to their success. They have learned to conserve their energy by minimizing the time spent in regret or complaint. Every event is a lesson to them, every person a teacher."
– Marilyn Ferguson

Great attitude; winning attitude; positive attitude—what's *attitude?* Attitude is a combination of your thoughts, feelings, and actions. So, for example, when your teenager grudgingly does a chore you have asked him or her to do: the *action*, the chore, gets done. But the attitude, the thoughts and feelings, consist of grumbling, excuses, and complaints. You feel drained by the experience. Something that should have been helpful has just been unpleasant. You know exactly what a bad attitude is. We've all experienced that.

What's a good attitude? A good attitude is being positive in the face of problems or adversity. It's making the best of a situation. It's enjoying yourself wherever you are, putting effort into everything you do. It's seeing something positive come out of a problem or a mistake, and being open to serendipity, where you are in the place you should be. Curb that desire to complain. If there's an unpleasant task that needs to be done, just do it, without complaining, because someone has to do it.

What does attitude have to do with *Smart Money*? You have the code ESCG™, the thoughts, and knowledge. Your feelings and actions have to align as well. I'm saying, have a positive attitude. Positivity attracts positive.

"Successful people are always looking for opportunities to help others. Unsuccessful people are always asking, 'What's in it for me?'"
– Brian Tracy

Affinity

"I've learned that people will forget what you said; people will forget what you did, but people will never forget how you made them feel."
– Maya Angelou

Affinity builds relationships, and that is one of our most important tasks. More affinity brings more relationships and possibilities. Affinity helps you get people to where you want them to be. People want to do things with people they like.

If you're asked your opinion, do you start with the negative? A major deterrent of affinity is criticism. So much of our training has been to criticize as a way of giving feedback. Criticism is thought to help people learn. People respond to rewards, incentives, and acknowledgement in training, more than they do to criticism.

How to use affinity? Acknowledge what is good, or close, or that the person tried, and offer suggestions. Curb your desire to criticize. Criticism often has a negative result. Instead of learning to improve, the person learns to shut down. Criticism is a hard habit to unlearn. When dealing with someone who has done something less than optimal, offer thanks and gratitude, and then a suggestion. People may be helping you, and it's your own attitude that prevents them from helping you. You are reacting to their criticism. Work on affinity.

Humility

Humility is to have a modest view of one's own importance. It does not mean low self-esteem. It's part of self-awareness. Arrogance is to be presumptuous and overbearing, and it breaks affinity. Humility is part of being authentic and listening to others—it's part of the glue that helps affinity—to act with compassion and understanding, appreciation and gratitude. Success is often a team effort, and there's a place for listening to the contributions of others.

If you want a window into someone, then watch how he or she treats others. I have been surprised at the grace and poise that many successful people have. They have a confidence in that they know things will eventually work out; so they don't have to sweat the small stuff because they have confidence in, and appreciation of, the people who know their stuff.

I've had some hard lessons and some blows to my ego. When times were tough, I had to do some jobs that I might consider beneath my skill set, but I needed to pay bills, and I did what I had to do. At one point, a recruiter told me, "You are going to make me look like a star." So I asked why, thinking he was impressed with my skills. His answer was, "Because you don't have any tattoos."

Honest hard work: that's a good lesson for everyone. What that job did was teach me things that I didn't expect. I've learned to appreciate how hard other people work. I had to learn skills I didn't realize were skills. I learned things about business logistics.

A very successful client was also one of the most modest. He was a very unlikely millionaire. He was a self-taught investor from a simple background. Just remember that arrogance stops you from learning. Humility allows you to learn and be open to the wisdom of others.

The opposite of humility is arrogance and I will say this about arrogance. When you refer to someone as arrogant, what you are likely evaluating is your belief in that person's competence. You may believe that his or her confidence is unwarranted or misplaced. When you believe someone is competent and brings value, you will refer to that person as brilliant or a genius. Steve Jobs, Elon Musk could be described as arrogant, but because they are considered so skilled and inventive, people dealt with their high handed and temperamental ways. People will respect and do business with people that are confident and competent. Arrogance is insufferable because it comes with other negative associations.

Energy

"The higher your energy level, the more efficient your body. The more efficient your body, the better you feel and the more you will use your talent to produce outstanding results."
– Tony Robbins

Raise your energy level. Depression brings your energy down. Financial worries bring your energy down. Health problems are often a symptom of low energy.

People are drawn to energy. Energy is like a currency. Bring it into your day. Bring it into your life. In simple ways, you can exercise, listen to upbeat music, go for a walk, or be in the sun. Do things that make you feel good. Sometimes those things are very simple. Look at gardens. Talk to children. Buy flowers. Be generous with compliments. Be grateful. Be kind. Make yourself an energy tea and drink it in. Have a positive vibration, and positive things will be attracted to you.

Be More Resourceful and Resilient

"It is during our darkest moments that we must focus to see the light."
– Aristotle

"Our greatest weakness lies in giving up.
The most certain way to succeed is always to try just one more time."
– Thomas A. Edison

Often, when you see success, you just see the results. You don't see what that person went through to succeed. Chances are, that person didn't have a smooth path or have everything handed to him or her. That person persevered and was resourceful and resilient.

We all have problems. Problems have solutions. Sometimes that problem presents a business opportunity. If you can, solve problems for yourself. I'm always surprised at how quickly people give up when they encounter a small problem. They go on Facebook and ask their friends to solve their problem. The solutions are there. Google. YouTube has videos on solving almost any problem you might have. With all these tools, many people still can't come up with a solution.

"Where do we enroll in Life 101? Where are the classes dealing with the loss of a job, the death of a loved one, the failure of a relationship? Unfortunately, those lessons are mostly learned through trial by fire, and the school of hard knocks."
– Les Brown

If you can provide solutions, then you are valuable. Ask for help *after* you've tried to solve your problem, not before. I'm not a computer person, and I've resolved computer issues using YouTube videos. I've done small home and car repairs. I find so much satisfaction in solving problems with my own skills or homemade solutions. I call it *MacGyvering*. When I solve a problem for myself, I feel good and resourceful. I've done small home, computer, and auto repairs that I didn't think I could do.

What have we done? We've shielded our children from problems. We've been taught failure is the worst thing. We've reduced resilience and resourcefulness as a whole. We've taken away opportunities to be brave, to face fears, to solve problems. Things can be hard, but part of parenting is to equip young people with life skills. We can't shield our children from life. Problems are a part of life, so be equipped with a solution-oriented attitude.

*"Success is not final. Failure is not fatal:
it is the courage to continue that counts."*
– Winston Churchill

"Problems are not stop signs; they are guidelines."
– Robert H. Schuller

Goals and Purpose

Realize most people don't set goals. A goal is *the object of a person's ambition or effort; an aim or desired result.* Setting a goal has you halfway to achieving it. Not setting a goal is a guarantee of not achieving it.

Have ways of measuring along the way. It can sometime be very discouraging if you're only measured by one big goal. Have some intermediary steps and ways of measuring success.

"It's not an accident that musicians become musicians, and engineers become engineers: it's what they're born to do. If you can tune into your purpose and really align with it, setting goals so that your vision is an expression of that purpose, then life flows much more easily."
– Jack Canfield

What's the difference between a purpose and a goal? Purpose is your *why* or *reason*. A goal is a tangible result. A goal is reinforced with a reason or purpose.

When do you find your purpose? Have you found yourself motivated? Do you feel that insights come to you, and synchronicity happens? Synchronicity is a *meaningful coincidence.* All things are possible, but not all things are probable. Have you found the improbable happening? When that happens, you are more closely aligned with your purpose. You will have more passion and enthusiasm for actions that are aligned with your goals and your natural interests. The right people will come into your life—more action, more opportunities, more contacts.

You may have one purpose. You may have more than one purpose. You may be singular in your purpose, at the expense of other things. You may be a business genius. How about multiple purposes: business, career, personal interests, parenting? Find your purpose. Know your purpose in each endeavour.

Acknowledgement and Appreciation

Acknowledgement is the act of expressing appreciation. Success isn't a singular pursuit. When you succeed, it's usually with the help of other people. Acknowledge the people who helped, supported, or contributed. You don't have to wait for success. Acknowledge the contributions, success, and actions of others involved in the stages to success. Where you see something positive or good, tell that person.

Celebrate All Success, Laugh and Play

*"The more you praise and celebrate your life,
the more there is in life to celebrate."*
– Oprah Winfrey

Sometimes success is a long haul. The steps can be hard and discouraging. Set intermediate goals, and when you meet them, celebrate. Reward yourself.

In talking to my daughter Brenna about playing outside in the snow, she said to me, *"Kids don't care about cold. You've been a grown up too long"*. I realized play is important. Kids play naturally. In fact, it is their job to play. Animals play when they are happy. A mistake I recognized later is that I didn't do anything to make myself happy. I kept telling myself when such and such happened, then I would reward myself. I just let work and the markets overtake my life and there was no joy. The overwhelming sentiment was negative and I came home to disappointment and frustration. This affected my ability to cope with stress, my health and I simply wasn't able to keep my head in the game. My desires for children kept me going. I rebuilt myself, but it took time. Mental fitness, happiness and positivity are an absolute requirement of achieving your goals. Do you play because you are happy or are you happy because you play? I am not sure. I just know play is important for health.

If it is raining on your parade, dance. Find someone or something that gives you encouragement and makes you laugh. A kind word means a great deal when you need it. You need balance in your life.

> *To laugh often and much;*
> *To win the respect of intelligent people*
> *and the affection of children;*
> *To earn the appreciation of honest critics*
> *and endure the betrayal of false friends;*
> *To appreciate beauty, to find the best in others;*
> *To leave the world a bit better, whether by a healthy child,*
> *a garden patch or a redeemed social condition;*
> *To know even one life has breathed easier because you have lived.*
> *This is to have succeeded.*
> – Ralph Waldo Emerson

Now and Delegate

Why do you procrastinate? You will do it someday. You don't have time. You are patient. You will do it when the time is right. Because you think you won't succeed. Because it is something you don't like to do. When things are perfect. You need to be in control. Stop making excuses. If you want to change, do something now.

NOW. Do you want to wait to be successful?   You want it NOW. So start NOW. When are you going to start? NOW. Action leads to action. Time lag leads to regret.

Learn to delegate. Get rid of the notion that you have to do everything. That you are saving money doing things yourself. Or that you are the only person that can do it right. If something is not getting done, you are quite likely the wrong person to do it. You can do so much more if you leverage the efforts of others. You are already delegating more than you think. If you take a taxi, you are delegating driving. If you are going to a restaurant, you are delegating cooking. Just expand the tasks you delegate. Write down one thing that you have put off for a long time and get someone else to do it. Then another and another. It may seem difficult at first, but you will explode with activity and action once you learn to delegate.

Progress for You

Now, I have shared my knowledge and life lessons with you. If you and I were to meet three years from now, what must have happened, both personally and professionally, for you to be happy with your progress?

I would like you to write your answer and date it, and put it in your calendar to read in three years. Put it in the calendar as if it happened; so, on that date, it pops up like a meeting with an agenda.

I've given you seeds of *Smart Money* wisdom. I share them with you to see them spread and grow. I see you increase your Earnings, Savings, Creation or Wealth and Giving. I see the benefits to you, your family, and your community; and, reaching out further, I see many people benefiting from your prosperity and generosity.

I have 100% confidence that you have the knowledge, attitude, and skills to succeed in your goals. I'm a work in progress. I've shared some of my experiences with you. I look forward to hearing your story and about your successes. I would like to thank you for your willingness to learn to grow and share.

"Life isn't about finding yourself. Life is about creating yourself."
– George Bernard Shaw

*"Keep your face always toward the sunshine,
and shadows will fall behind you."*
– Walt Whitman

*"All our dreams can come true,
if we have the courage to pursue them."*
– Walt Disney

*"There are only two ways to live your life. One is as though nothing is
a miracle. The other is as though everything is a miracle."*
– Albert Einstein

Peace, Shalom, Inshallah, As-Salaam Alaikum, Namaste, Slainte, Ciao, Salut, Servus, Aloha, Pura Vida, Sawubona, Vanakkam

Getting Results

Words to look up:

What is the most important thing for you to get the results you want?

What is the first thing you are going to do NOW?

What is one thing that you have avoided that you can delegate?

If you and I were to meet three years from now, what must have happened, both personally and professionally, for you to be happy with your progress?

Testimonials

"Janet dealt with high net worth sophisticated investors, seeking her expertise in order to protect their investment portfolio in tempestuous times. She has the ability to analyze asset classes from strategic perspective and guide her clients profitably with lower risk. Personally, Janet reaches out in business and makes friends. Her integrity, warmth and intelligence shines around the world."
- Shan Saaed, Chief Economist, IQI Global, Malaysia Economic and Investment Analyst

"Janet is the smartest advisor that I ever spoke with. Janet doesn't think outside the box. She doesn't know there is a box."
- Elia Draicchio, Encryption and Security Specialist

"Janet posed very creative financial solutions and opportunities. She proposed a transaction during the financial crisis that was ultimately done by Prem Watsa. Her signature portfolio construction, shorting bonds and investing in high yield, netted above average returns witl lower volatility and an inflation hedge. My only regret is that I didn't invest more with her."
- Firoz Shroff, Real Estate Investor

www.ingramcontent.com/pod-product-compliance
Lightning Source LLC
Chambersburg PA
CBHW072347200326
41519CB00015B/3695